IMAGINARY AUDITION

Imaginary Audition

Shakespeare on Stage and Page

HARRY BERGER, JR.

University of California Press
Berkeley • *Los Angeles* • *London*

University of California Press
Berkeley and Los Angeles, California

University of California Press, Ltd.
London, England

© 1989 by
The Regents of the University of California

Library of Congress Cataloging-in-Publication Data

Berger, Harry.
  Imaginary audition: Shakespeare on stage and page / Harry
Berger, Jr.
    p.   cm.
  Bibliography: p.
  Includes index.
  ISBN 0-520-06558-1 (alk. paper)
    1. Shakespeare, William, 1564–1616. King Richard II.
2. Shakespeare, William, 1564–1616—Criticism and inter-
pretation—History.   3. Shakespeare, William, 1564–1616—
Dramatic production.   4. Richard II, King of England, 1367–
1400, in fiction, drama, poetry, etc.   I. Title.
PR2820.B47   1989
822.3'3—dc19   88-29087
                                                            CIP

Printed in the United States of America
1   2   3   4   5   6   7   8   9

An earlier and much shorter version of Chapters 1 and 2 and
portions of the Prologue and of the Introduction to Part One
appeared as "Shakespeare on Stage and Page: Against Theater-
Centered Criticism," published in *Journal of Literary Criticism*
[Delhi] 3, no. 2 (1986). An earlier version of Chapter 4, along
with passages from the Prologue, Chapter 5, and the Epilogue,
appeared as "*Richard II,* III.ii: An Exercise in Imaginary
Audition," in *ELH* 55 (1988): 755–96.

For

Caroline

Cynthia

David

with love and in strictly alphabetical order

❖ ❖ ❖ ❖ ❖

We scarcely ever hear the words we utter.

Noam Chomsky

Contents

Preface

I could not have written this book had it not been for the wonderful colleagueship, support, encouragement, and resistance to my flakier ideas offered over the years by my dear friends Audrey Stanley, Michael Warren, and Paul Whitworth. They listened to my tirades against theater with varying shades of unbelief, horror, patience, and derision. Their example, their precepts, and their amused chuckles had a lot to do with the modifications I made in my initially simplistic view of relations between reading and performance. Thanks to the great success of Shakespeare Santa Cruz, founded by Professor Stanley, I have been blessed by the opportunity to study with and learn from the experts. And thanks to the Shakespeare Focused Research Activity at Santa Cruz, directed by Professor Warren, I have been able to test some of the ideas in the book before informed audiences from whom I received much constructive criticism.

Also very important in helping me think through the theoretical framework of the book during the past few years have been conversations with, and criticism from, other friends: Beth Pittenger, Marsh Leicester, Diane Manning, Louis Montrose, and Margreta de Grazia have contributed much to the process of reeducation involved in trying to write a book. I am also deeply grateful to Stephen Greenblatt, Margaret Ferguson, Jonathan Goldberg, and Stephen Orgel not only because they have been personally supportive and encouraging but also because it is chiefly their efforts, along with those of Montrose, to revitalize early modern studies that inspired me to return to problems of theatrical representation after I thought I had ended up in an intellectual blind alley.

Like everything else I have written, the ideas and interpretations contained in the following pages were aired and tested

ix

under the demanding conditions of the contact sport called teaching. I began to think seriously about the Henriad in 1978, when I taught the first of a series of undergraduate and graduate seminars on the tetralogy. By their articulate skepticism, their demands for clarity, their willingness to entertain and experiment with what must have seemed weird notions, and their imaginative development of ideas many of which I'm sure I have stolen, they have placed me under an obligation it is a pleasure to acknowledge. I think especially of Diane Manning, Heather James, Lisa Lowe, Donald Beggs, Kenneth Reinhard, Catherine Gimelli-Martin, Richard Martin, Katherine Eggert, Oliver Arnold, Lindsay Kaplan, and Brian Myers, because there is no question in my mind that they are the chief victims of my thievery.

The final shape of this book owes much to the discernment, generosity, and sympathetic criticism of Jonas Barish and Edward Snow, the two readers for the Press. The final shape of the manuscript that preceded the book owes everything to Charlotte Cassidy, whose extraordinary combination of typing skill and editorial intelligence I defy anyone to match. The precarious journey from manuscript to book was negotiated chiefly through the good offices of Doris Kretschmer, acquisitions editor for the Press; Rose Vekony, who oversaw its production; and Jane-Ellen Long, whose attentive and judicious copyediting is responsible for many improvements in style, clarity, and meaning. Special thanks go to Peter Harris, head of the Educational Resources Department of the Graduate Center of the City University of New York, not only for permission to use his photograph as a jacket illustration but also for his generous spirit of cooperation in making the photograph available. Thanks also go to Professor William Elton for allowing William Shakespeare and myself to share the imaginary space of Mr. Harris's photograph with him. Finally, thanks go once again to Wallie Romig, supervisor of the Cowell College steno pool, and to her staff, Marianna Alves and Janette Crutch, for the willing and gracious provision of services without which an aging academic (or a young one, for that matter) could not get off campus before midnight, and to the Committee on Research of the University of California for the support that enabled me to finish the book.

PROLOGUE

From Stage to Page

More than twenty years ago Sigurd Burckhardt complained of the prevalence of "an odd superstition . . . that nothing can be part of Shakespeare's intention that cannot be communicated directly across the footlights." He dismissed as nonsense the idea that because Shakespeare "was a 'man of the theater'" we should expect the performance of any play to be "the unmediated thing itself" rather than "an interpretation, derived (it is to be hoped) from a very careful reading of the text by the director and the actors." His point was that actors and directors were not doing very well as interpreters and needed more help from "those who have the time and patience to *read* Shakespeare, down to the minutest detail." [1] Today this opinion would be laughed out of court by partisans of stage-centered criticism who are not only true believers in the "odd superstition" but also active opponents of the sort of "careful reading" that produces pages of commentary on minute details no theater audience could be expected to unpack without stopping the play and starting an in-house seminar.

Since 1966, when Burckhardt's words were written, those partisans have mounted an active campaign against the anti- or nontheatrical tendencies of the armchair approach that dominated Shakespeare studies for several decades in this century. Imbued, perhaps, with the spirit of the 1960s, and riding the crest of a back-to-theater movement in England and America, they have put the "time and patience" faction on the defensive by premising that the kind of interpretation playgoers practice under the conditions of actual performance should provide the model and criteria that govern reading. In the work of its most determined polemicists, J. L. Styan, Richard Levin, and, more recently, Gary Taylor, stage-centered criticism hews pretty closely to the narrow view characterized by Burckhardt—though Taylor, at least, is more interested in Shakespeare's text than in his intention.[2] The proponents of the New Histrionicism, as it may be called, argue that reading is irresponsible unless it imitates playgoing, and in its strongest form this argument establishes the empirical experience and psychology of playgoing as the exemplar whose privileges and constraints are to be reproduced in armchair interpretation.

My aim in this study is, first, to challenge some recent versions of New Histrionicism and some of the theories that enable it, and, second, to illustrate an approach to reading that provides an alternative both to the reductive practice New Histrionicists advocate and to the excesses of armchair interpretation which (in my opinion) they properly criticize. If the critique of New Histrionicism in Part One appears unrelievedly negative, it is because I intend it to serve a space-clearing function, which is to say that my own interpretive position will be composed out of the dismantled and reorganized premises of theater-centered criticism. This position will then be developed and illustrated in Part Two, chiefly through a reading of a single scene of Shakespeare's *Richard II,* the second scene of act 3. The reading will be introduced and contextualized by a selective account of my view of the play as a whole, and it will be interrupted by occasional digressions that register both my debts to and my disagreements with other approaches, in particular the metapoetic and metatheatrical approaches whose proponents find the theatricality of *Richard II* so seductive. I have chosen to focus on *Richard II* partly because that aspect of the play allows me to keep the question of theater in the foreground, but partly also because I consider this book to be a kind of prolegomenon to a larger study of the Henriad on which I am currently at work. In the Epilogue, I try to bring together the critique of New Histrionicism and the reading of *Richard II* in some generalizations that touch on the problematic relation of Shakespeare's text to the instituted theater process in terms of which he wrote. The remainder of this Prologue will be devoted to a quick sketch of the genesis of my present position and to an outline of its differences from New Histrionicism on the one hand and conventional armchair reading on the other.

I tried to formulate the basic commitments of the position in two earlier essays. In the first attempt, which was unsatisfactory and has been justifiably criticized, I depicted the problem as a conflict between text and performance or reading and audition (which includes spectatorship).[3] My argument was that the performance/audition medium imposes constraints that limit interpretive response to the Shakespeare text, that these constraints are ideological, that the author of Shakespeare's texts represented both the limits of performance and its ideological implications, and that this representation is more accessible to readers than to playgoers.[4] The simplistic and tendentious privileging of reading over audition that weakened this argument was caused by misplacement of the polarity, and in my second formulation I noted that the conflict is not between reading and audition but between two interpretive emphases within reading, one that promotes the constraints of performance/audition to the status of norms that should govern *literary* response, and one that doesn't.[5] Calling these two orientations of reading "stage-centered" and "text-centered," I argued on the same grounds as before for the priority of the latter, but I also insisted that text-centered reading should remain "parasitical on stage-centered reading" because "it must always attend to the ways any theatrical interpretation . . . reflects interests, values, powers, dangers, privileges, and constraints embedded in the very structure of theatrical relationships as they were institutionalized in Shakespeare's time and are represented by his texts" (60).

In that essay, however, I glossed over an important distinction between the psychological constraints that playgoing imposes on interpretation, and the theatrical circumstances (the "structure of theatrical relationships") that reading must attend to. Reading can ignore the constraints while attending to the circumstances, or it can ignore both. Since it is obvious, thanks largely to Richard Levin's critique, that much armchair interpretation falls into the latter category, a simple distinction between stage-centered and text-centered reading is inadequate. I propose instead a tripartite scheme: reading that respects both the constraints and the circumstances; reading that respects the circumstances but not the constraints; and reading that ignores both. My focus in this book is on the first two. I shall call the first the *theatrical* model of stage-centered reading and the second the *literary* model of stage-centered reading.

Those who operate the theatrical model do not seem aware of the existence of the literary model, and there is no reason why they should be, since it is a little invention of my own. In earlier essays I have made gestures toward describing it,[6] but the interpretive sample that occupies Part Two demonstrates a particular practice which I haven't yet discussed and which gives this book its title: the practice I call *imaginary audition.* Though the sample is framed as a confirmed armchair interpreter's challenge to the New Histrionicism, it involves an attempt to reconstruct text-centered reading in a way that incorporates the perspective of imaginary audition and playgoing; an attempt to put into play an approach that remains text-centered but focuses on the interlocutory politics and theatrical features of performed drama so as to make them impinge at every point on the most suspicious and antitheatrical of readings.

The tripartite scheme outlined above suggests that the basic distinction premised by New Histrionicism is both inadequate and invidious. The contrast between the reader as academic critic (relegated to the third of the three categories) and the ordinary intelligent playgoer in the street is only mildly caricatured by reconceiving it as a contrast between the Slit-eyed Analyst and the Wide-eyed Playgoer: the former subtle, suspicious, cynical, ironical, elitist, deviant, neurasthenic, forever skulking about in his or her armchair; the latter simple, vigorous, normal, trusting, true, attuned to the larger-than-life effects of Shakespeare's Human Opera, and, above all, *there*—in the presence of the real thing, face to face with the veritable play-in-itself. In this view the ideal reading imitates, or pretends to imitate, the experience of playgoing. But New Histrionicism has never been very consistent in conceptualizing the figure of the playgoer. I think it is safe to say that the critic's playgoer, to paraphrase Walter Ong, is always a fiction—virtual, imaginary, implied, and so forth—that serves to allegorize the conditions and experience of performance as the critic formulates them.[7] This is also true of the playwright's audience: whether one characterizes it as the virtual audience implied by a particular play or set of plays or dramatic conventions, or as the audience function constructed by various kinds of instituted theater process, the collective playgoing subject is a role with specific historical parameters.

One of the problems with the New Histrionicism is that it has not as yet bothered to distinguish between the two concepts of critic's and playwright's audience, much less try to correlate them. Another problem, shared with much reader-response criticism, is that its proponents are neither consistent nor precise in distinguishing between the virtual and the empirical playgoer.[8] A third problem, one which (as we'll see) especially troubles Gary Taylor's approach, is that New Histrionicists often find it convenient or necessary to posit a playgoer innocent of the effects of what Richard Levin calls "the Age of the Reading." In this age the construct of innocent playgoer is likely to be very much a fiction, or a hyperbole, since it presupposes a presuppositionless experience in theater—the experience of one who always sees a play (as if) for the first time—and thus ignores the influence of the institutional complicities of a literate culture. But, by the same logic, such a construct would have been less hyperbolic in Shakespeare's time, when the scope of literacy was more limited and when even literate playgoers may not have had easy access to texts. If we add to this the often attested fact that the theater process was unruly enough to make playwrights as well as Puritans complain, we may well wonder whether the author of Shakespeare's texts wrote strictly and only in terms of the attentiveness or understanding he could expect from those audiences. If he wrote *for* them, he may also have written *against* them and *about* them. In short, there is reason to suspect that the Shakespearean critique of theater targets precisely the system of innocent playgoing which the New Histrionicism sets up as a paradigm. And, as I hope to show in Part Two and the Epilogue, *Richard II* is notable for its sharp focus on that system, for the way both the text and the protagonist represent, model, and mock their innocent auditors.

PART ONE

AGAINST NEW HISTRIONICISM

Introduction

The bias of critics who pledge allegiance to the theatrical model of stage-centered reading is never more evident than when they proffer ecumenical embraces to armchair interpreters. Thus although J. L. Styan concludes *The Shakespeare Revolution* by insisting that actor and scholar "will teach each other," each modifying the other's illumination in "a process of infinite adjustment," he proposes this marriage in a way that favors the theatrical spouse: "any unnatural separation of reader and playgoer implied by" periodicals and books devoted to Shakespeare criticism "will suggest a critical inadequacy, a failure to integrate current knowledge." Styan agrees with John Russell Brown "that the play on the stage expanding before an audience is the source of all valid discovery. Shakespeare speaks, if anywhere, through his medium." Styan will admit, apart from such approaches as M. C. Bradbrook's study of stage conventions and G. Wilson Knight's visionary theater, only a few scholarly impediments to this marriage:

> There is no question but that the actors spurned most of the scholarship and criticism which seemed to lead readers away from the aural and visual heart of the play experience. The schoolroom lacks the correlative aura of the theater, and, for students, criticism which is not stage-centered has been the source of much enervating treatment of Shakespeare, the liveliest of playwrights. However, some of the more fruitful research of recent years has been in the history of performance, reconstructed through promptbooks and contemporary reports.
>
> The intense semantic scrutiny of the new critics undoubtedly worked wonders for our understanding of poetry . . . but it stumbled badly when confronted with drama.[1]

3

Styan's view of the contrast is refreshingly forthright. His no-hard-feelings dismissal of "intense semantic scrutiny" is based on a strict construction of the medium Shakespeare "speaks" through which appears to rule out the possibility that close attention to the medium Shakespeare writes in could produce anything but invalid discoveries. Such a narrow view of stage-centered criticism might be empirically justified as a reaction to large quantities of armchair interpretation, but as a theoretical position it is vulnerable to Harriett Hawkins's attack on "critical books" that refuse to be contaminated by their "counterbooks."[2] A much more flexible approach, and one that shows considerably more subtlety in dealing with the text, has recently been attempted by Philip McGuire in *Speechless Dialect.*[3] McGuire uses the phrase "open silence" to denote a character's "failure or refusal or inability" to speak at a critical moment (xix) with the result that important knowledge is missing, the text is per se indeterminate, and the particular value(s) of the silence can be established only during performance. The open silence thus epitomizes the limits of the text, and though McGuire's is surely one of the most balanced, persuasive, and promising treatments of stage-centered reading to come along, though it offers several opportunities for a rapprochement between the different interests of theatrical and literary reading, it remains canonical.

McGuire speaks for many stage-centered critics when he warns of

> the limits inherent in the approach that has dominated the study of Shakespeare's plays since at least the time of Dr. Johnson. Those who utilize that approach, which has reached its zenith in this century, seek to understand Shakespeare's plays by treating the words that Shakespeare wrote as if they were elements of a literary text rather than parts of a dramatic script. They take assumptions, concepts, and processes of analysis developed for and appropriate to works written to be read by individuals in silent solitude and apply them to works designed to be heard and seen by people who have come together as a group in public in order to see and hear a play.
>
> (xviii)

Through a series of interesting and imaginative readings of passages that contain "open silences," McGuire tries to demonstrate the inadequacy of the basic premise of the literary approach, the premise that the text is not a script but the "abstract principle of order underlying the multiple (often confusingly varied) performances of the play" and that performances are developments of the initial or primary "state of the artistic system" which "(as playtext) should yield all knowledge essential to the play and . . . enable us to predict specific states that the play will assume when performed" (132–33).

Instead of this commitment to the completeness and causal efficacy of the text, McGuire proposes "a new ontology" that will "accommodate rather than deny" performative "freedom and multiplicity" by treating the play's mode of being as "an ensemble of various possibilities that may overlap and even conflict with one another." The playtext is accordingly reduced to the status of a "*verbal . . . construct that describes that ensemble*" (138–39). Along with that he follows Norman Rabkin's (but also Burckhardt's) precedent by proposing "the principle of complementarity" as "the cornerstone of an epistemology capable of accommodating . . . multiplicity" and contradiction (142).[4] Since this is a theory in which performative use determines textual meaning, a reading of the playtext can never do more than lay out the ensemble of possibilities that underlie and enrich the selectivity of performance: "Each actualization of a specific possibility during a performance excludes other possibilities that are not only equally valid but also equally capable of providing necessary information about the play"; hence the excluded possibilities "contribute to our understanding of the action performed" (145).

Neither McGuire's defense of the theatrical approach nor his critique of the literary approach is sufficiently stringent, because what he offers is not so much a theory as a set of metaphoric assertions based on, and borrowing, concepts from the history of science: the shift from literary to theatrical "ontology" and "epistemology" is depicted on the model of the shift from classical to quantum physics.[5] Too much energy is devoted to justifying this laborious development and translation of the analogy (none of which was needed to make the fairly obvious points McGuire makes), and in a way the analogy is self-defeating. Just as Newtonian physics remains valid for the analysis of a special range of phenomena within relativity physics, which in turn remains valid at a particular scale or level of analysis, so, one might argue, the principles of text-centered reading may validly "accommodate" the "freedom and multiplicity" of *literary* performances. Literary as well as theatrical performers can—and often do—treat the text as the verbal construct of an ensemble of overlapping and conflicting possibilities. Perhaps because he takes his own ecumenism more seriously than Styan does his, McGuire does not present a strong enough case for the *invalidity* of text-centered readings that are at least prima facie antitheatrical and unstageable. And it is only by confronting such a strong position that proponents of the validity of text-centered readings can submit their views to an adequate test.

More aggressive positions have been staked out by polemicists concerned primarily to encourage reform of what they see as the irresponsibility of much academic interpretation, its irrelevance to or disdain of theatrical experience, its failure to police itself, and its inadequate methods for testing and refuting critical conjectures. Richard Levin, Harriett Hawkins, and Gary Taylor have each taken on some of these issues with admirable energy. Hawkins's argument explicitly relies on and in many places intersects that of Levin. Taylor endorses their critiques but finds that they "do little to replace the edifice being torn down" and proposes to do this himself—"to replace the modern emphasis upon interpretation with a kind of critical hedonism, the study of drama as a 'superior amusement,'" a study that analyzes the moment-by-moment effect on playgoers of a scene from *Julius Caesar,* a character in *Twelfth Night,* a production of *Henry V,* and a scene from *King Lear.*[6] To my knowledge, Taylor's is the first attempt to work out an alternative model of stage-centered interpretation in response to Levin's critique. I shall therefore consider the critique in Chapter 1 and Taylor's model in Chapter 2. My aim in the former is not merely to show that the conceptual framework that underwrites Levin's attacks on slit-eyed analysis falls apart under scrutiny but also to suggest that while our current view of the conditions of writing and performance in Shakespeare's time lends no support to that framework, it offers considerable comfort to the kinds of reading he criticizes. In dissecting Taylor's account of wide-eyed playgoing I hope to demonstrate that it relies on a set of premises whose actual structure is the inversion of what he claims it to be, and the aim of the demonstration is to appropriate that structure as the basis of the method of imaginary audition to be illustrated in Part Two.

I note in conclusion that although I consider Hawkins a tougher-minded and more interesting critic than Levin, I choose to concentrate on the latter because Hawkins does not present a specific brief for theatrical versus literary reading. Hers is a general methodological critique of criticism and performance. Often, in fact, her emphasis runs counter to Levin's, because it is on the complexity of response Shakespeare's plays call for, the difficulty of writing about that complexity, the failure of critics to surmount the difficulty, and the consequent need for more effective methods of critical self-refutation. Nevertheless, as I noted, she leans heavily on Levin's work and had earlier applauded his "devastating criticism" of "whole treasure troves of nonsense recently stashed away in scholarly publications" and "his lethally serious (yet always witty) attack on the methodological assumptions that lie behind" many of the "preposterous statements" he puts on parade in *New Readings vs. Old Plays*.[7] I am (with reservations) more sympathetic to the criticism than to the methodological attack. But Levin at least makes explicit the way that premises supporting the theatrical model may be deployed against the categories of reading he finds misguided, and he therefore presents a confrontable position.[8]

ONE

Richard Levin's Critique of Slit-eyed Analysis

Levin's critique in *New Readings* is based on three premises that mutually implicate each other and function as a system of interdependent variables. They are the playwright's intention, the actability of any interpretation, and the traditional interpretive consensus. In the first section of this chapter I shall describe and analyze the system, disarticulating the premises in order to show that none of them stands up by itself.

The basic principle of Levin's attack on the "new readings" (thematic, ironic, and historical) that challenge the traditional views of Renaissance plays "held, so far as we can tell, by virtually all spectators and readers down to the present time" (ix) is

> that the dramatist wanted to be understood by his audience, that he wanted them to grasp his intention and respond to it appropriately, and therefore took some pains to ensure that they would. . . . If we can trust him, then we ought to approach these plays with the assumption that they are to be treated as "straight"—that is, as meaning what they seem to mean—unless they contain clear indications to the contrary. . . .
>
> Another important consequence of our principle is that we can and should trust not only the playwright and his play but also the response which this play has evoked in most viewers and readers. For if he wanted to be understood and was at all competent, then their response would correspond to his meaning. It would follow, therefore, that whenever an established interpretation has grown up around a play that has been experienced by many people over many years . . . , it is very much more likely to be very much closer to the truth than some brand new reading.
>
> (143–44)

9

Thus, for Levin, "the most reasonable hypothesis" about a play of this period, the one adopted by "the overwhelming majority of viewers and readers down to the present," is that it is "a literal representation of particular characters engaged in particular actions." This representation produces the "actual dramatic experience" of audiences and "should be presumed to embody the play's primary meaning" (199, 204, 202).

Actability is the implicit mediating criterion between playwright's intention and audience consensus. Hawkins puts the following question to a recent reading of *Antony and Cleopatra* that concludes "that Antony never loved Cleopatra": "how on earth is the actor portraying Antony supposed to inform everyone in the audience that he is only faking it and, simultaneously, convince everybody on stage . . . that his passion is real?" "After all," she continues, "the public nature of the drama requires that motivation be established, and necessary information got across to the audience with maximum impact, in the course of only two or three brief hours on the stage." These and similar reflections lead her from actability to the other two criteria. She finds it obvious

> that Shakespeare, who showed no interest in publishing the text, could not have taken it for granted that anyone in his audience would see *Antony and Cleopatra* more than once, much less study the script in advance of seeing it, or subsequently read—and re-read—it to ponder its subtleties. Nor could he have assumed that the truth about Antony's motivation would finally manifest itself unto generations yet unborn. To succeed as a playwright in the commercial theater, he was obliged to write for the general public, and against the deadline set by a single performance; and both these contingencies suggest that, so far as his major meanings and effects are concerned, some credence may be given to the historical record of responses to his plays, including critical disagreements about their meanings and effects.
>
> (*Devil's Party,* 110–11)

On the basis of these three criteria both Hawkins and Levin argue that "the burden of disproof" (Hawkins) is on the new readers who reject the consensus interpretation, and that the logical consequence of rejecting the time-honored consensus is to accuse "our greatest dramatist" (Levin) of failing to get his meaning across.

Levin's argument, augmented by its logical presuppositions, runs as follows. Playwrights intend to write plays (not poems) and intend to convey specific meanings in the way plays (not poems) convey meaning, and they want those meanings to be understood by audiences in the way audiences understand during performance (not in the way readers understand while reading in the study). If the playwright is competent his wish will come true and audiences will interpret his meaning accurately. Shakespeare was competent. Therefore whatever interpretation the majority of playgoers agree on must have been the one he intended. This circular argument is not so much disingenuous as it is bumptious, since the "intending dramatist" is transparently a character created by Levin to validate his approach, or at least what he takes to be the right approach, and to invalidate the others. Of Levin's three criteria, this is in fact the one on which stage-centered critics show least agreement. Both Taylor and McGuire, for example, take issue with the intention thesis:

> Traditional criticism is based, fundamentally, on intention; studies of audience response are based on effect. Usually the analyst of response assumes or asserts that the author's intention can be inferred from the response his work produces. But this is patently false. If it were true, no play could fail. It would be more accurate to say that every dramatist constructs a hypothetical audience, and that the success or failure of his intentions depends on the relation between his real and his hypothetical spectators.
>
> (Taylor, *Moment by Moment,* 158)

> Did Shakespeare consciously craft the open silences in his plays? Since we lack such documents as Shakespeare's various drafts of each play and his notebooks, there is no way to answer that question definitively. Perhaps, perhaps not. . . . Our uncertainty becomes greater if we keep in mind G. E. Bentley's demonstration . . . that what a playwright of that era wrote was generally the property of the acting company for whom he wrote it. Thus, as far as we can tell, what we today call Shakespeare's plays were not then thought of as "his" in the modern sense of the term. . . . Indeed, it is conceivable (but, again, not demonstrable) that it was not Shakespeare's ideas that were enacted during an open silence

> but the ideas of another member of the company . . . or even ideas that were . . . formulated collectively and that remained subject to change. (McGuire, *Speechless Dialect*, xxii–xxiii)

The question of the author thus remains an open silence. Levin's thematists, ironists, and occasionalists all fill the void with their own versions of "intending dramatist," and so do I.[1] But the difference is that we are not part of the consensus—or, according to Levin, that we have rejected the consensus and constituted ourselves as a second audience, a small elite of hermeneutical adepts claiming access to textual secrets withheld from the deceived majority.

Exactly who *is* this majority? Granted that the burden of disproof is on the new readers, exactly what is the consensus interpretation they are supposed to try to disprove? The argument from consensus is as slippery as the argument from intention. Let's eliminate the intending dramatist, since "he" is no more than a rhetorical device for reinforcing the majority opinion. Then it must be consensus alone that determines a play's "apparent" or "primary" meaning, and it must be on the basis of observed consensual practice that Levin decides plays should "be construed literally," should "be taken at face value." But is there only one consensus and "face value" or are there many? I can't imagine that Levin imagines the consensus to march through time in so monolithic a phalanx—Levin's Army—as his references to it imply. Yet he fails to provide any statistical or other documentation that would give us a sense of diachronic change and synchronic variation in the consensus. Nor does he define the limits of tolerance within which critical disagreements and changes of fashion may still be resolved into that consensus.[2] Stage histories and histories of criticism show continual revision and conflict, as I am sure Levin knows better than I. So I suspect that Levin produces his consensus retroactively in precisely the same manner as he claims ironists and other New Readers produce their deceived majority. First the new readings are identified, classified, and targeted, then the old readings are marshalled up against them and the enduring, unified, consistent order of Levin's Army generates in its image an enduring, unified, consistent version of *the* apparent, primary, literal, and face-value meaning.

Levin's Army is of course no mere chimera; it has more substance than the intending dramatist. Its purpose comes into view when, for example, Levin claims the following authority for the assumption that plays should be taken "straight": "it describes the expectation or mental 'set' which audiences actually bring to plays when encountering them for the first time (at least up to very recently), and which dramatists, even ironic dramatists, count on when writing them" ("Hazlitt," 143). The parenthetical phrase alludes to a major feature of Levin's argument: his trenchant discussions of the problems caused by the professionalization of literary studies, the proliferation of journals entailed by the publish-or-perish imperative, the rise of New Criticism and "the Age of the Reading" (passim, especially 1–5 and 194–207). As Stanley Wells observes, before Dowden and Bradley "the great names in Shakespeare criticism" were "primarily men of letters, only secondarily teachers and lecturers," but "by far the larger part of the mass of Shakespeare criticism produced since Bradley's time has been academic, some of it obviously originating in the lecture room, and some of it still more restricted in appeal, being published in learned journals that are read only by a limited number of specialists."[3] Levin's Army includes the generations of playgoers, learned or unlearned, who are or were unspoiled by the fall into the Age of the Reading, and it also includes those unspoiled by the Age of Reading that made plays available in another medium. It does not include, for example, the romantic critics, who "usually divorce Shakespeare from the theater or ignore the fact that he wrote plays."[4] It includes all who gather together under the slogan "What may be digested in a [performed] play" and who follow their leader's charge against the outlaw readings that threaten them with indigestion. This, incidentally, suggests not only the strategic function of the actability criterion but also its weakness. Stage-centered critics often seem to underestimate the good actor's ability to work up and/or stage complex interpretations, and they often ignore the influence of particular styles or traditions of acting on what counts as an actable interpretation. Since those styles both form and are formed by audience preferences, actability and consensus reinforce each other in a purely relativistic way that may have as little to do with what the author intended as it has to do with the range of alternate and potentially stageable interpretations inscribed in the playtext.

Thus I conclude that the argument for the superiority of this theatrical model of stage-centered reading is not persuasive. It depends for its validity on the mutual implication of three criteria each of which, when disarticulated from the others, turns out to be highly suspect. This is not to say that the specific critiques and the general project of reform undertaken by Levin and Hawkins are not effective and salutary. I find myself sympathetically concurring with many of their witty and sometimes devastating commentaries, though Levin's case would have been stronger had he not exercised the art of snippetotomy with such exuberance: too many of his decontextualized examples are presented in the worst possible light. He didn't need to marshal up Levin's Army and its adjuncts to deal with such straw men. But the Army serves another purpose. It allows him *categorically* to invalidate the nonconsensual approaches he proscribes without having to discriminate among examples, and it thus precludes the possibility that some examples of ironic or thematic practice may be more promising than others.

Is there an alternate rationale or charter myth, one that could authorize the practice of Levin's outlaws rather than that of his Army? Suppose, for example, we lean on the different implications of the following two statements, the first by Levin and the second by Hawkins: "the dramatist wanted to be understood by his audience, . . . he wanted them to grasp his intention and respond to it appropriately, and therefore took some pains to ensure that they would"; "To succeed as a playwright in the commercial theater, he was obliged to write for the general public, and against the deadline set by a single performance." If I take Hawkins's statement to suggest that the dramatist was *obliged* to write for the public whether he wanted to or not and that he was obliged to entertain and please them, I might be inclined to question Levin's assumption that he wanted to be understood by *that* public or to confine himself to intentions which *that* public could grasp and respond to appropriately. At the very least, I might wonder whether he *expected* to be understood. The questions open up a view of the dramatist's relation to his medium and audience which differs sharply from Levin's bland hypothesis. I note in passing that Levin has very little to say either for or against the major studies of Shakespeare's use and representation of theatricality. Such names as those of Barton, Burckhardt, and Calderwood do not appear either on his Index or among the critics he finds most trustworthy. Yet it is precisely in the studies of Shakespeare's relation to and representation of his medium that Levin could find the sort of counterevidence that would help him test his hypothesis.

The view that emerges from those studies is one with which we are very familiar. We know, for example, that though dramatists were relatively well paid they lacked control over their compositions; that publication in the folio format which then signified "serious" literature did not occur until Jonson's *Workes* in 1616 and the 1623 Shakespeare Folio; that playwrights were employees of acting companies and had to tailor "the literary product to the qualities of the actors, the design of the theater, and the current conventions of production."[5] And to their audiences:

> One might expect the playwrights to carry more weight with their condemnations [of audiences], and they were certainly more eloquent: Nashe attacked audiences in 1592, Heywood in 1595, Marston in 1597, 1603 and 1604, Chapman in 1599, Beaumont in 1607 and 1609, Fletcher in 1609 and 1613, Dekker in 1609 and 1610, Webster in 1611, Middleton in 1613, Carew in 1630, and Jonson at frequent intervals throughout his career. But all their attacks were on bad judgement rather than behavior, and cannot therefore be looked on as reasonably disinterested. A few playwrights sometimes went to the other extreme of flattery, but with no more sign of disinterest than when they condemned.[6]

As Jonas Barish has demonstrated in his remarkable study, the antitheatrical prejudice was not monopolized by Puritans. Jonson's attitude toward "'the loathèd stage,'" his "caustic view of the stage practice of his day," may have been unusual in its violent expression but even "in such a born man of the theater as

Shakespeare . . . we find elements of deep suspicion toward theatricality as a form of behavior in the world."[7] The playwright's
ambivalence, it should be emphasized, was occasioned not merely
by constituents of theatrical experience as symbols of general experience but by problems in those constituents themselves—
problems with players, audiences, patrons, censors, playhouses,
pirates, and Puritans.

From the kind of theater Shakespeare worked in, his discussions and representations of theatricality, his dual role as poet on
the one hand and playwright/player on the other, and the different kinds of patronage associated with these roles, Alvin Kernan
has made a notable attempt to construct a hypothesis about
Shakespeare's attitude toward the theater:

> The paradox, represented by the image of the poet as magician, of
> art as mere illusion and high vision, was forced upon Shakespeare
> by an irresolvable conflict between his Renaissance conception of
> poetry as a superior kind of truth and his material situation as a
> professional playwright working in the public theater where plays
> were only transitory shows. Every aspect of that theater, from his
> own professional status as a provider of entertainment for pay to
> the structure of the playhouse itself, reminded him of the contin-
> gency of his own art within a reality more problematic and more
> durable than itself.[8]

As the last sentence suggests, much of Kernan's evidence is drawn
from the *Sonnets,* which he reads less as autobiography than

> as depicting in a much more general way the experience of a tran-
> sitional generation of poets from an amateur to a professional
> status, and from [aristocratic] patronage to the marketplace as a
> source of support. Whatever longings Shakespeare may have had
> to be a fashionable and courtly amateur . . . the *Sonnets* are fi-
> nally . . . an apology for the necessity of working in the public
> theater. . . .
>   The *Sonnets* justify theater. . . . But the step from the great
> house to the theater is taken . . . with great reluctance at leaving
> the golden past, and with grave doubts about the nature and value
> of the new medium in which the poet must now realize his art. As
> the Muse of the theater, the Dark Lady promises as much pain as
> pleasure, at least as many lies as truth, and perpetual ambigu-
> ity and uncertainty. It was exactly in this problematic way that
> Shakespeare seems to have understood his dramatic art, and his

plays contain a long record of a continuing effort to deal with and explain a medium which remained always something less than fully satisfactory.   (48)

If the full potential of the playwright's art were to be realized, . . . it would have to be in some pure theater of the imagination, free of the limitations of real actors, stages, and audiences, and such a theater could only be created within the play itself. . . . [But] Shakespeare, as if his imagination could not free itself from the conditions in which he actually worked, regularly presented internal theaters which were deeply entangled in and limited by the circumstances of actual production.   (135)

These plays-within-plays, Kernan comments elsewhere, always involve "an upper-class . . . audience viewing with varying degrees of scorn and condescension . . . a play . . . put on by lower-class players, either amateur or professional." He argues that this represents "an aristocratic artistic attitude towards the public drama . . . with which Shakespeare partly identified and which at the same time he opposed and criticized." Kernan speculates that the reason Shakespeare "never shows us an entirely ideal audience" may be that he thought "he could make his points about audience response and responsibility by showing what an audience should not be. . . . But it is also necessary . . . to take seriously the fact that the playwright who pleased his audiences so well that he became rich and famous by doing so expresses in his plays only suspicion and doubts of an audience ranging all the way from groundlings, like Sly or Caliban, . . . to great nobles like Theseus and the prince of Denmark."[9] One could infer from this that for Shakespeare any theater audience was either potentially or actually "what an audience should not be." This would be the standpoint not of an aristocrat but of a poet, and especially of the poet who wrote the *Sonnets*.

Kernan's hypothetical author directly challenges the one constructed by Levin to validate the criterial status of the playgoing majority's interpretation(s) and thus to confirm the superiority of the theatrical model of stage-centered reading. For if Kernan's Shakespeare intended to be successful, he dissociated this from another intention based on the expectation that neither actors nor audiences could be counted on to do his plays justice.[10] It isn't necessary to conclude from this, as Levin does, that the dramatist set out to deceive his audiences and concealed more complex meanings behind simpler ones, though I can imagine a streak of auditory voyeurism in Kernan's Shakespeare. Nor, however, is it necessary to conclude that the Shakespeare who wrote the *Sonnets* carefully circumscribed his explosive manipulation of language within his *literary* performances—that the language of the plays must be conceived of as insulated from such linguistic bravura simply because they are plays, even though they often exhibit a density of language effects comparable to that of the sonnets. Kernan's Shakespeare—and mine—knows how to write successful plays while still indulging his indomitable zest for literary *jouissance,* and, like many other authors, takes pride in that double accomplishment.

Two other hypotheses contribute to the construct of a duplicitous author. The first can be stated quickly because it is, or should be, obvious and because it involves a phase of production about which not much is known: the original audience for which the Shakespeare text was written consisted not of the theater audience subsequently conscripted into Levin's Army but of the author's collaborators and competitors in the rehearsal process. Even if a play was accepted in final form before rehearsal began, the fact that it was written for a repertory company meant that rehearsal was still an interpretive factor: the playwright's interpretation of his literary material was affected by his knowledge of the currently available acting material. The less we know about rehearsal the more we can imagine. We can, for example, imagine that company in-jokes and private allusions found their way into the text, that revision of the script was part of the process, that territorial warfare was a constant factor, that questions of revision could therefore be tense and produce both compromises and defensive maneuvers that altered the text, and that these considerations were not inevitably harmonious with, or subordinated to, the motive of succeeding with Levin's Army.

The second hypothesis interposes yet another audience between the author and the Army, an audience most stage-centered critics seem to have overlooked. It is the audience bound to authors in the collaborative process of interpretation Annabel Patterson has described as "the hermeneutics of censorship."[11] The hypothesis behind Patterson's study of censorship in early modern England presupposes a view of authorial intention that must at least complement Levin's and supplement Kernan's. The hypothesis of duplicity suggested by Patterson, however, points in a different direction from the one suggested in the rehearsal/ repertory hypothesis, for it joins the author and the theater audience in a conspiracy against the mediating audience of censors. Patterson argues that in this period "'literature' . . . was conceived in part as the way round censorship." It was the medium in which "the institutionally unspeakable makes itself heard inferentially, in the space between what is written or acted and what the audience, *knowing what they know,* might expect to read or see" (63). This union between author and audience might at first glance give the stage-centered critic cause for celebration. The only problem is that it suggests that ironic, thematic, or occasionalist responses may from time to time be expected of Levin's Army.

Patterson views "the prevailing codes of communication, the implicit social contract between authors and authorities, as being intelligible to all parties at the time, as being a fully deliberate and conscious arrangement" (17), and she distinguishes her approach from more structurally oriented Marxist and Foucauldian accounts by its greater emphasis on agency and putative intention:

> It is a central part of my project to show how the historical condition of an era of censorship united writers and readers in a common interest as to how interpretation in fact worked, how it could be carried out in any given sociopolitical situation, how the interaction between writers and readers could be formulated in ways that were intelligible (in law) and useful (in politics).   (7)

> What this book offers is an account of one period in which there was clearly and widely understood a theory of *functional* ambiguity, in which the indeterminacy inveterate to language was fully and knowingly exploited by authors and readers alike (and among those readers, of course, were those who were most interested in control). Functional ambiguity frees us somewhat from more radically skeptical conclusions about indeterminacy in language and its consequences for the reader or critic; unlike other theories,

> it does not privilege either writer or reader, or eliminate either. It is hospitable to, and indeed dependent upon, a belief in authorial intention; yet it is incapable of reduction to a positivistic belief in meanings that authors can fix. Indeed . . . [this study shows] that authors who build ambiguity into their works have no control over what happens to them later.   (18)

Patterson stakes out a territory very different from that claimed by Leo Strauss in his study of the concealed esoteric text.[12] She studies censorship, rather, as a historically conditioned "system of communication" and as a cultural ambience, a set of understandings that pervasively affect writerly awareness and practice (15–16). In this system "ambiguity becomes a creative and necessary instrument, a social and cultural force of considerable consequence" (11), and of course the instrument was wielded by dramatists as well as other writers. Patterson explores *King Lear* as a test case because what we know "'about' . . . its 'sources', its circumstances of production, its most plausible sociopolitical and cultural contexts, not only fails to resolve its internal ambiguities but actually seems to create new contradictions, to highlight new ambivalences in the text" (59). Her exploration leads her to question the esthetic motive prevailing among the proponents of the double-text theory, or at least to challenge the polemic defense of it Gary Taylor makes in *The Division of the Kingdoms* against extrinsic explanations (60–64).[13] A comparison of the political evidence with topical allusions and echoes widely scattered through the play leads Patterson to infer that the debate centering on James's proposal to unite the two kingdoms influenced the play, that *King Lear* was indeed a "deeply [and safely] ambiguated" response to "the Union controversy, but one deliberately shaped by its author's understanding of the hermeneutics of censorship" (71). Patterson's tempered and tentative conclusion deserves relatively full citation because it speaks so powerfully against the oversimplified view of author/audience relations adopted by stage-centered critics. If, she argues,

> we posit that both the earlier and the later versions of *King Lear* were conceived by Shakespeare in response to constitutional and cultural excitement, to a political discourse in which familial rela-

tionships had acquired an intense metaphorical freight, . . . we may not be any closer to resolving *King Lear*'s internal conflicts of sympathy and polity, but we may be closer to understanding why they exist. And to read the play not only as a fully meditated (and slowly evolving) response to major political events and statements but as a contribution to them . . . is not, surely, to reduce its status as art. Rather, it may help us to replace the concept of literary transcendence, which seems to be currently exhausted, with the more rigorous concept of intellectual independence; that quality which Shakespeare manifests more powerfully than any of his contemporaries, but which in him, no less than in them, was partly the consequence of living with censorship. (73)

The critique of New Critical estheticism may be extended to the stage-centered concept of *theatrical* "transcendence." Patterson's study develops a genetic hypothesis radically different from the one presupposed by Styan, McGuire, Hawkins, and Levin, a hypothesis that supports the image of a Shakespeare whose practice demanded auditory voyeurism and the promotion of discrepant awareness in his diverse audiences. The consequence of living with censorship may be added to other consequences: living with the egotism and varying competences of players, with the conditions of public theater, and with audiences that were far from ideal. Why shouldn't writing for, and with, and against all audiences—and that includes the primary audience, the repertory company—be modeled on writing for, and with, and against censorship?

Writing for censors is writing for readers, and this applies to plays as well as literature. G. E. Bentley states that by 1574, plays were already being *read* in the Revels office.[14] And though we may assume that expressions in various media are at all times subject to forms of censorship, the period investigated by Patterson is unique for the obvious reason that the climate and institutions of censorship were being changed by the use of the printing press. Printing, like other institutions and practices, has its own life, logic, and structural contradictions. The same properties encourage literacy, revision, sectarianism, and the conflict of interpretations on the one hand, and censorship on the other. As Joel Hurstfield observes, what differentiated the Tudor government from all those which went before was the emergence, for the first time, of a mass medium, the printing press, an instrument of enormous power. . . . We know . . . that the government held a tight grasp on Parliament, the pulpits and the printing press and strove, not always successfully, to silence the expression of dissentient opinion, in both the spoken and the written word. The government fully recognized the danger of dissent and fought it with a powerful body of writers who poured out, often under Cromwell's direction, a stream of pamphlets whose sole object was to justify the king's ways to men.[15]

Hurstfield recognizes that the "long-term effects of the invention of printing . . . were, and still are, ambiguous," and he points out that "the voice of dissent used the printing-press" no less than the government did (70). But if we properly consider *long*-term effects, dissent is only a symptom of a more complex set of structural changes. First, the expansion of the crown into the king body politic during the Tudor regime gradually empowered rival institutions. "Sovereignty" came to be identified "not with the King alone or the people alone, but with the 'King in Parliament'"—a corporation "from which the body politic as represented by Parliament could never be ruled out."[16] Second, the rival institutions had the peculiar property of empowering interpretive elites centered on the writing and reading of law and legislation, not to mention the communities centered on the reading, interpretation, and effectual rewriting of Holy Scripture. In different but coalescing ways, the House of Commons, the common law, the civil law, and Puritanism were reading and writing movements. Never mind that they began with traditional intentions, and pursued reactionary and antiquarian strategies, and used their texts logocentrically, as the Puritans did when they brought God's word and book into the home. The logic of alienation governs textuality and typography as well as "the fetishism of commodities." Thus, as Patterson clearly perceives, though censorship is one source of certain kinds of ambiguity and though it stimulates the habit and skill of ambiguous writing, "authors who build ambiguity into their works have no control over what happens to them later." Ambiguity may be inflamed by the power of print and print literacy to release textual power, or it may be quenched by the reactive censorship imposed, for example, by those who wish to protect the clarity of scripts meant for the stage from the texts that smolder beneath them.

Perhaps Harriett Hawkins is right to insist that Shakespeare "showed no interest in publishing the text," or perhaps, if the text was company property, he wasn't able to publish it; perhaps he transcribed and saved a duplicate set of foul papers; perhaps most of them were lost or burned, and the few that remained were entrusted to Heminge and Condell; perhaps. Perhaps he did expect that at some point readers would be able to "study the script," to "read—and re-read—it to ponder its subtleties." Or perhaps not. Perhaps Heminge and Condell are only echoing his advice and sentiment in the First Folio when they urge "the great Variety of Readers" to "Reade him, therefore; and againe, and againe: And if then you doe not like him, surely you are in some manifest danger, not to understand him." Or perhaps they aren't echoing his advice. I think the rules of the game change when the Age of Reading makes the plays available in the same medium as the sonnets and when, owing to the spread of literacy and the institution of literary studies, the plays are read and studied more than they are seen and, indeed, are often seen in order to provide "enrichment" for the practice of reading and studying. For better or for worse, the Age of *the* Reading exposes the *jouissance* of the Shakespeare text to the *jouissance* of what Stanley Fish calls "interpretive communities" but what Levin more realistically treats as interpretive *elites*. This may or may not be a bad thing, but at any rate it strikes me as anachronistic or antiquarian to turn the clock back to a time when plays were not expected to be read, much less studied.

"Whoever—and however many Whoevers—wrote Shakespeare's plays intended them to be performed, seen, and heard." In this form, the intention statement is trivial because unfalsifiable. It would be better to generalize the statement and localize intention: "Any text culturally recognized as the script of a stage play looks as though it 'wants' or 'intends' to be performed, etc.; that is, it appears to be intended to produce such an intention in its readers." I have no objection to this version of the formula so long as it is stated as a description rather than as a disjunctive imperative ("a script is *only* intended to be performed"). For, in practice, performance entails interpretation. Actors interpret the script to themselves and each other with a view to presenting their interpretation to audiences, who interpret their interpretation. When readers or playgoers respond to the text they respond to an interpretation: their own, the editor's, the critic's, the actors', or merely the interpretive force of the presuppositions that inform the context of any activity and shape expectations. Plays are now read as texts, not only as scripts, and there are literary as well as critical performances. Plays, then, like other texts, appear to be intended for interpretation, which includes performances in various media; and, like other texts, their apparent "intentions" are dissociated from those of their authors and subject to continual cultural revision. If there was a Shakespeare who could not anticipate the consequences of print culture or of the institutionalization of reading and literary studies, that is not a Shakespeare we should have to conjure with, or conjure up, today. But we still do, and in the next chapter I shall conjure with the Shakespeare Gary Taylor conjures up.

TWO

Gary Taylor's Defense of Wide-eyed Playgoing

"Shakespeare's reputation," Gary Taylor writes, "has since the Restoration always rested, and continues to rest, largely on the power of his plays as reading-texts," and though critics "may argue—justifiably, in my opinion—that the plays can only be fully appreciated in and through performance, . . . the fact remains that many people who have never seen them performed satisfactorily, or at all, have derived immense pleasure from merely reading them" (*Moment by Moment*, 27–28). This almost even-handed treatment of reading and playgoing, qualified only by the phrase "justifiably, in my opinion," occurs more than once in Taylor's book. Though he promises to substitute "critical hedonism" for interpretation, he acknowledges his indebtedness to "'new' criticism" as well as to other approaches (vii). His interpretive practice is often subtle and probing, and his critical passages target productions as well as readings, judging both from the standpoint of a theory about the limits of audience comprehension. But for the most part Taylor endorses the negative attitude of Levin and Hawkins. The critics whose stage-centered argument he deems justifiable are seldom mentioned, and his programmatic statements usually display a chip-on-the-shoulder attitude toward literary critics, whom he dismisses, in an admittedly "caricaturistic" manner, as ego-crazed deviants to be segregated from normal playgoers and also, presumably, from the many normal readers who derive "immense pleasure from merely reading" the plays (5–9, 150–53, 161, 166–69, 230–39).

The plan of *Moment by Moment* is stated modestly: it is to analyze "the pleasure of moments," and it is not yet "a study of audience response," only the necessary preliminary to that study.

25

To pursue this project Taylor has found it necessary to eschew "brilliant and subtle new interpretations" in order "to explain how everyone arrived at the old ones" (12–13). Though this recalls Levin's consensus theory, Taylor is careful not to reduce "everyone" to the unanimous phalanx of Levin's Army, and on several occasions he shrewdly analyzes the various factors producing differences of response within and between audiences. Nevertheless, he manages to bring this analysis round to a qualified reaffirmation of consensus, as when he asserts that "differences between spectators are minute, by comparison with the differences between spectators as a class and readers (especially critics) as a class. Sometimes these differences matter little; but sometimes, as with *Henry V,* they are crucial" (160). As the parenthetical phrase suggests, the class difference is hierarchical. Of the book's four interpretive studies, the chapter on *Henry V* presses hardest on the difference because, although "both the play and its protagonist have been applauded by centuries of audiences," in recent decades the play has stirred up controversy that Taylor attributes to the "disparity between the pleasure of spectators and the displeasure of readers" (112).

In this chapter, Taylor's case against text-centered reading is most fully stated in terms of the actual constraints on the playgoer's perception. His plan is "to observe and analyze the contemporary pleasure of a succession of audiences" at a single production of *Henry V*—Terry Hands's 1975 Royal Shakespeare Company version—"and thereby isolate and analyze differences between reader and audience responses in a play where those differences are especially striking" (2–3). Taylor's conclusions are based on a variety of data which include observation of several audiences, informal interviews, records, reviews, and some fine-tuned interpretation contrasting performance effects with text effects. The lore of perceptual psychology gives him his "control." He argues that the playgoer's pleasure is conditioned by the limits of short-term memory and other aspects of attention and that such focalizing strategies as selective amnesia exhibit the sciencelike operation of a "principle of economy": "an audience will accept the simplest possible hypothesis which explains the data" (157). This principle underlies his assessment of the

RSC production's successes and failures, while failures in literary criticism are traced to violations of the principle. The following five examples will illustrate the method Taylor employs in developing his titular contrast between readers and seers.

One: Taylor concludes a stimulating account of the obscenities in the English lesson, and the implications of Catherine's awareness of them, with the following summary: "a reader, and more specifically a critic, is unlikely to enjoy the joke because on the page puns lose their spontaneity and social context" (124).

Two, on the difference between reading Fluellen's dialect and hearing it: "In the theater Fluellen is a born Welshman; on the page we are perpetually reminded of Shakespeare making him Welsh. On the page he loses the illusion of an effortless unconscious spontaneity" (128).

Three: the same contrast holds for the distinction between naive and tendentious jokes (which Taylor borrows from Freud). After observing that "tendentious jokes stand up to reading" and repetition better than naive jokes, he argues that when the written text represents dialect by "phonetic distortions of spelling," it "is perpetually reminding the reader of the creation of the joke, and since the characters have themselves no desire to be funny, we attribute that act of creation to the author." This "spoils for readers the naïveté of the joke," so that they become aware of the author's "tendentiousness . . . at the expense of his characters" (129).

Four: in Henry's "Once more unto the breach" aria, the imperatives

> reaching for you from the page seem clumsy and undramatic. In the theater the army mediates between Henry's imperatives and the audience. . . . But for a reader the army does not exist at all. For a reader the empty space of the theater itself does not exist, and that great volume is even more important than the army in mediating between us and Henry, for the emptiness must be filled by the actor, and by filling it with the swell of his voice he impresses upon us his power, his magnificence.   (138)

And, five: of "the French King's invocation of his nobles" in 3.5, Taylor insists that although it is "magnificent in the theater" it "makes no impression at all on a reader, for the simple reason that it's a list." The reader "can see no ascending or innate significance in the items themselves, and indeed there is none"—until the actor gives each item weight and structures the list "toward a climax. . . . The emptiness of the speech for a reader is a measure of its fullness for a listener" (141).

It might occur to readers that Taylor's view of their naiveté is tendentious. He gives them very little credit for skill in imaginary audition or visualization. None of his characterizations of the limits of reading fits either my experience or my practice, and I can't tell whether or not I am freakish in that respect since Taylor does not share with me any principles of reader psychology comparable to those he adduces for audiences. The possibility of imagined performance, of stage-centered reading that submits to literary rather than to theatrical controls, finds no place in his polarization of readers and seers. Yet Taylor's own readings of the language lesson and several other scenes are finely imagined. They help at least one reader to a vivid apprehension of some of the ways performance can interpret the complexities of text. His account of the language lesson reduces my inability to "hear" or respond to the jokes as if delivered. I suspect that Taylor's ideal deprived reader is as inexperienced in theater as I am. Yet when he mentions the army and the empty space and great volume of the theater that do not exist for that reader, they begin to exist for this reader. Taylor helps me imagine the effect of Alan Howard's passionate Henry aiming his Harfleur aria at me, and the effect of the resonance of the French king's voice giving life to the list of nobles. Even as Taylor belittles the reader's ability, he increases it by his forceful literary portrait of a production. I can confidently predict that if *Moment by Moment* succeeds with other readers as it did with me it will render obsolete the theory of reader impoverishment which it is its purpose to endorse. And if the new army of Taylor-trained readers were to rise up en masse from their armchairs and march off to the theater, knowing what they know, would this change in the data base call for any revision in the principles of playgoing psychology?

I have many substantive disagreements with Taylor's interpretation of *Henry V,* as well as with his conduct of the procedure illustrated in the previous pages. But since an adequate critique would require me to lay out my own counterinterpretation not only of *Henry V* but also of the *Henry IV* plays, a task that would divert me from an analysis of Taylor's general orientation, it cannot be undertaken here. Suffice it to say that he demonstrates in this chapter more than the others what he means by his claim that "the proper study of audience response must confine itself to empirical audiences," as opposed to the dramatist's or critic's hypothetical audience (158). Taylor's interpretive practice in the other three chapters does not rely to the same extent on the scaffolding provided by this empirical appeal to the psychology of actual audiences. In fact, as I shall now try to show, his claim is not compatible with his practice, because all the latter requires is the critic's hypothetical audience and a generalized model of performance conditions which is as easy to imagine as to experience directly.

In the closing sentences of his chapter on *Henry V* Taylor executes a rhetorically sinuous attack on the subclass of "abnormal" critics, moving from an apologetic and concessive posture to a whipcracking finale: in order to describe "a complex succession of complex moments" he will be forced

> to advocate one interpretation of a particular work at the expense of another; at which point the approach to drama through audience response will have become (what it is often accused of being) simultaneously "reductive" and "subjective." Or, to put it another way, this approach to drama will then be capable of reducing the self-defeating, self-indulgent clutter of conflicting and incompatible interpretations, by demanding that the subjective responses of individual critics be subordinated to the objectivity of the audience as a whole. (161)

What guarantees "objectivity" and unanimity are the common perceptual limits on information-processing, attention, and memory, along with the operation of the principle of economy evinced by the tendency of spectators to "apply fairly similar criteria" in the interpretation of theatrical data (157).

One of the more interesting consequences of Taylor's invidious contrast is that it testifies to the richness and complexity of a text which is overwritten from the standpoint of performance and the playgoer's limited perceptual capacities. Interpretive decisions and reductions are forced on the playgoer by those limits. For the reader, who "perceives" the fixed signs rather than the moving phenomena of performance, the "laws" of perception impose different constraints that play a smaller role in interpretive decisions. Reading demands more voluntary "discipline" in representing the phenomena that have been displaced from signifier to signified, in imagining and taking into account the absent constraints that theater imposes. Taylor insists that "when a critic notices . . . parallels or presumes . . . mental juxtapositions" that would not be obvious in theater "he is under some obligation to consider whether an audience would naturally make them; if not, he should say so, concede that his interpretation depends upon giving an extra theatrical emphasis, by no means inevitable, to certain parallels, and explain exactly how theatrical emphasis could be achieved" (153). Even as Taylor acknowledges that the text licentiously offers interpretive possibilities which are non- or antitheatrical, the stern command to "explain exactly" has the force of a disabling challenge. As the embodiment of the perceptual laws and enforcer of the principle of theatrical economy, the spectator is always right. The audience is an Office of the Revels, a superior court, to which critics (like directors and actors) submit their work for censorship and judgment. From this spectatorial judiciary Taylor excludes the critic because of his "abnormal" responses, his lack of the common touch, his disdainful "refusal to become part of the audience, to submit to the collective will" (9). It is therefore to be expected that in his role as defender of the people Taylor does not find the exact explanations he requires and that the Taylorian audience judges critics guilty of untheatrical conduct: loath to prune their interpretive hedging, withdrawing limply into a textual happiness overrun by parallels and juxtapositions, stumbling on melons plumped up with irony, critics succumb to "*a compulsion to compare,* having (as the spectator does not) the leisure and the means to do so" (150).

Although Taylor accuses critics of generating a "self-defeating, self-indulgent clutter of conflicting and incompatible interpretations," he seldom goes so far as to accuse them of irresponsible fantasy in their negotiations with the text. On the contrary, his argument is that the critic's "abnormal familiarity with the text" (6) makes it hard for him to turn away "from the text to its performance, away from contemplation of the essence toward evaluation of a particular manifestation of that essence" (8); the "abnormal intensity of his attention . . . enables him to perceive what others do not—including, perhaps, things he was never meant to perceive" (6). Granted that "perhaps" archly signals understatement, the phrasing allows the inference that those "things" may have been there to perceive but that the critic makes too much of them, and indeed most of Taylor's comments on the sins of criticism target its tendency to privilege the complexities of the textual "essence" at the expense of an actable and easily comprehensible manifestation. Thus the complexity and the potential or apparent unstageability of the Shakespeare text qua text are never in question.

Taylor and I might well agree that a passage of text lends itself to a complex interpretation because it contains conspicuous echoes, parallels, and similarities that encourage juxtapositions. We might also agree on what the passage means, or on whether its possible meanings are incompatible, conflicting, or reconcilable. We might even agree that since "no audience will make" the juxtapositions (150) this reading could not easily be accommodated within the principle of perceptual economy. Our argument would then be whether the reading should be ruled out on those grounds. Why should the text of a competent playwright encourage interpretations that are theatrically gratuitous? Does the disproportion between essence and manifestation mean that the playwright is abnormal and self-indulgent, even self-defeating or at least prodigal, in producing a surplus no audience was meant to perceive? Why should I, poised at the crossroads between the generosity or generativity of the text and the perceptual limits of the playgoer, sacrifice the first pleasure to the second? Since there is much virtue in If, why should I read a play as if I can only take in what I could when actually watching it rather than pretending to watch a play that contains everything I see in the text? Why should we oblige critics to prune their hedges rather than obliging directors and actors to try to represent them on stage? Why is it up to critics rather than directors and actors to "explain exactly how theatrical emphasis could be achieved"? Above all, what if they try and fail? Does that invalidate the imagined performance of a stage-centered interpretation developed under and for conditions of reading rather than those of theater? And does it invalidate it for all time, or only for so long as it remains uncongenial to prevailing conventions of theatrical interpretation?

These questions are addressed to the three basic assumptions of Taylor's argument: first, that the criterial status of actual performance conditions is self-evident; second, that any interpretation that does not conform to those conditions must be non- or antitheatrical and violate the Shakespeare text (by treating it as a text rather than a script); third, that a valid interpretation must match or reproduce the experience of actual playgoers. The issue for me is whether Taylor has made a compelling case for these claims, and in the final section of this critique I shall argue that he hasn't.

Taylor begins with a radical distinction between the innocent playgoer and the fallen critic. In his introductory chapter he makes much of the distinction between the first and subsequent viewings of a play (6, 9–12), and though the distinction is developed in the value-neutral terms of the psychology of attention it is tendentiously framed. In our first encounter "we tend to shape ourselves to fit the object" and to "*accommodate* ourselves" to the "experience"; "by subsequent encounters we seek to *assimilate* that experience, to master it, . . . to incorporate it into our own system, . . . to shape the object to fit ourselves" (10). First we open ourselves to the other, and then we destroy its otherness by mastering and consuming it. The purpose of this rhetoric is to convert the distinction into another weapon in the attack on critics: "It is in these subsequent encounters that the biases and motives of the critic's profession may most seriously distort his perceptions" (11). Taylor nevertheless goes on to add a vaguely concessive gesture, "We want both the impartiality of innocence and the subtlety of experience in our responses," and to assert that although his book will be "almost entirely concerned with our initial responses" he includes in that category "any subtlety which *could* be perceived in that first encounter" (12). This loophole, as we shall see, will become important.

The criterion of innocence is the basis of a significant practical restriction imposed by Taylor, his caveat against the fallacy of "reading a play backwards," in which "readers and audiences, returning to the play, may be tempted to presume what they should discover, by bringing to bear at once the information they have acquired through previous exposures to the play" (166). He describes this fallacy as follows:

> "Reading a play backwards" is a species of anachronism: it transfers something out of its proper place in a temporal sequence, into a time where it does not belong. A play, being a temporal sequence, is also subject to other species of anachronism. . . . For our previous experience of the play involves not only information, but also the emotions attendant on that information. A spectator who has been often moved to tears by Lear's sufferings may regard the Lear of I.i with an excessive, sentimental, anachronistic sympathy, which has no source and no function in that scene, at that time. . . . But if anticipation may produce anachronisms, so may memory. The better the critic knows the play, the closer he comes to a simultaneous perception of all its parts, which will allow him to ignore the chronological imperative of performance. If, in *King Lear,* the critic can simultaneously perceive, in detail, scenes IV.vii and I.i, then the latter is no longer a distant background to the former; instead, two foregrounds are juxtaposed. His own knowledge of the whole has destroyed the dramatist's organization of perspective, and, as a consequence of his omniscience, he is confronted with a series of contradictions, which must be intellectually resolved into true or false, when in fact the dramatist never intended A and non-A to be juxtaposed.[1]

Earlier in the book Taylor had commented on "the selective amnesia which affects an audience's interpretation of any given moment," and he cited this as "central to an understanding of dramatic unity and structure, and of the differences between audiences and readers" (46). In the above passage, however, he seems to *advocate* selective amnesia: the proper attitude for anyone who has read and knows a play or has seen it more than once is *to pretend* to be ignorant of the play and to be seeing it for the first time. Anyone who has fallen into repetition or reading must assume the part of innocent playgoer however many times he or she has seen or read the play. This implies of course that reading backwards is possible because there are texts; there is another way to experience the play because there is another state in which the play exists, and that other state must be screened out along with that other way. Therefore the playgoer *pretends* that the play being seen as if for the first time only exists as it appears in theater—a temporal sequence, a succession of moments—and this appearance is its reality: "In one very real sense a performed play is . . . pure appearance" (16). Thus the innocent playgoer and the play-as-only-temporal-sequence are interdependent fictions in a system of virtual representation.[2] This system is given a privileged place in an asymmetrical opposition whose second term is a system comprised of the experienced playgoer, the reader, and the critic; and the written text.

If this position as I just described it is Taylor's, it would be easy to demonstrate that his text *Moment by Moment by Shakespeare* deconstructs itself. The system he demotes to the negative or supplementary term has to be posited so that it can be bracketed or ignored in order to produce the privileged system. And in a more immediate manner the former provides the enabling condition, the ground of possibility, of the latter: Taylor's own acts of interpretation and exclusion employ all the resources of the system he criticizes in order to argue for the priority of the system he promotes.[3] If the privileged system is no less imaginary, no less a critical construct, than the other, there is no prima facie reason why reading backwards or any other way can't be made to contribute to the imaginary audition of temporal sequence. But although Taylor's argument at times seems vulnerable to the set of moves I just made, my description is reductive and the moves correspondingly facile. His position is more complex, his defense of it more intelligent, and, above all, he is not so naive as to base his argument on a psychologically improbable (if not impossible) fiction of innocence. Another glance at his discussion of anachronism will disclose a slightly different agenda.

Taylor adduces Robert Heilman's *This Great Stage* as a New Critical example of the fallacy of reading backwards. Heilman's practice, Taylor claims, abstracts the play's "themes" and "documents" its "verbal and intellectual preoccupations" as if they "exist outside time, and can be extracted from the moment" (168). But Taylor then proceeds to sketch out a middle ground between the extremes of innocence and New Criticism. "No one would deny that the play eventually dramatizes" the themes abstracted by Heilman, but the "'innocent' audience could hardly be expected to appreciate" them at first sounding or to remember those "modest soundings" later, when "these themes have been made manifest." And yet

> no one who knows the play can read or hear the first scene again without perceiving and indeed savoring the aptness of the first restrained articulation of each theme. In each case critical "anachronism" genuinely increases our immediate pleasure in and appreciation of a moment of the author's play. . . . We savor the first snatch of melodies which will eventually develop into major musical themes. The "innocent" playgoer could not be conscious of such touches, but they do I think nevertheless contribute to his or her total response to the play. If we are not conscious of such details . . . then they cannot influence our sense of the action's specific meaning: meaning is the product of conscious interpretation. But the alliteration of ideas does strongly contribute to our sense that the action *has* a meaning. (168–69)

The enclosure of *innocent* in quotation marks is significant. It both flags the virtuality of the imaginary playgoer and displaces that figure from its privileged position. The meaning the innocent playgoer merely intuits can't be as articulate as that produced by the "conscious interpretation" of someone who knows what to expect and whose pleasure will thereby be both more intense and more refined. The innocent playgoer is now clearly a hyperbole invented as a counterweight to the gravity of academic "omniscience," and these two mighty opposites create a polarized field within which readers and playgoers can find their bearings. While Taylor urges them to move from one pole toward the other, he also suggests they stop short of the angelic pole.

Who, or what, then, is the new ideal playgoer? Taylor gives us more than a clue when he announces that the result of a long analysis of the first four scenes of *King Lear* is the conclusion that our feelings toward Lear have shifted from antagonism to sympathy:

> A rather bathetic conclusion, no doubt, to sixty pages of analysis. But that is precisely my point: that such conclusions do not matter, that in themselves they tell us less than nothing about the greatness of a work of art. What matters, what gives us pleasure, is the emotional and intellectual richness of the individual moments that contribute to those conclusions, the process by which we arrive at them, the experience of which they are the transitory culmination. . . . Conclusions can only be reached by an analysis of moments, and conclusions are only valuable in relation to the analysis of subsequent moments.   (229)

The "us" and "we" tend to conflate Taylor's analysis of the "richness of . . . moments" with the pleasures of playgoers so that his ideal playgoer turns out to be an informed reader—informed, that is, by assimilation both of Taylor's analysis of moments and of his method of analysis. The Taylor-trained reader has learned how to make alterations that eliminate academic waste material and fit the text to "the chronological imperative of performance." The innocent playgoer who reached Taylor's "bathetic conclusion" intuitively, experienced a pleasurable glow of Meaning, and thereupon exclaimed on the greatness of Shakespeare's art would fall far short of the ideal. A clear sense of what Taylor offers, allows, and expects of the informed playgoer may be gathered from that portion of his sixty-page analysis of *King Lear* which deals with the Fool's language in 1.4, and especially with his "Have more than thou showest" speech (195–206).

In this excellent reading, for me the high point of the chapter, Taylor persuasively demonstrates that the ambivalences in the speech are "designed not to enlighten, but to bewilder" (200), and that the Fool's message is genuinely indeterminate: "The auditor struggles to keep hold of the Fool's commandments, waiting for the key which will suddenly unite them—and instead, when we expect the solution, the Fool produces nonsense and anticlimax" (201). Nevertheless, there is enough discernible sense in the speech and there are enough glints of "relevance to the larger context" to tease auditors and readers into looking for a coherent message. Readers have more time to succumb to the temptation: "A reader can govern the speed and direction of his reading, as an auditor cannot; he has time to puzzle out the lines, time to attempt to relate them; he needn't worry about storing the sequence in his memory while he awaits the key, because for the reader the text is itself an infallible memory, available on demand" (202). After canvassing the words and phrases of the speech for their possible meanings, Taylor concludes that Shakespeare "perpetually promises and perpetually denies definition" (204) and that the coherent explanation which best fits the larger context is "anachronistic, a symptom of 'reading the play backwards'" (203).

While Taylor shows that the bewilderment of the innocent playgoer is an appropriate response to the Fool's language, a response that matches Lear's "This is nothing, Fool," he also shows that the Fool's "nothing," like Cordelia's, muffles some conspicuously relevant "somethings" and that to be aware of both the promise and the denial of those meanings can greatly enrich the moment-by-moment response. In order to produce the interpretation that in his opinion best accords with what the text can (and should) convey in the normal tempo of performance, he avails himself of privileges specific to reading. He slows the text down and sometimes brings it to a standstill. He puzzles out the lines, consults several commentaries, and checks conclusions against later and earlier parts of the play, reading backwards in order to determine how much anachronism can or can't be tolerated. And of course his major thesis commits him to the sin of textual dismemberment or, to put it more benignly, the art of snippetotomy. Thus after extracting a scene from the body of *Julius Caesar* and devoting thirty-four pages to it, he apologetically defends this procedure: "This limitation is inherent in the study of moments . . . and I am quite willing to concede that it is a serious limitation, involving as it does an inevitable distortion of the work of art," but it is "certainly no *more* distorting than the standard [academic] alternative, and it at least has the advantage of remaining closer to the artistic experience" (48–49).

"Artistic experience" is a phrase fuzzy enough to include both the portion of text whose meaning or staging Taylor analyzes in detail and the response of the playgoer from whose limited perspective the analysis is made. Taylor's ideal playgoer is one who will attend a performance of *King Lear* armed with Taylor's reading—with insights accessible only through reading—and who, while carefully avoiding the fallacy of reading backwards, will appreciate the vibrant interplay of promise and denial, the pattern of conspicuous exclusions, which is inaccessible to the innocent playgoer. He or she will "savor the first snatch of melodies which will eventually develop into major musical themes" but will at the same time feign just enough innocence to control the tendency to anachronism so as to savor each moment most fully. The innocent playgoer is thus the product of a complex and sophisticated interpretive reduction; "innocence" is produced by the experienced playgoer's strategy of conspicuous exclusion.[4]

If, then, the innocent playgoer is a hyperbole, a strategic construct, so also is its correlative, the play reduced to pure temporal sequence. Any performance that isn't sheer improvisation is the citation and recitation of a text, and even a playgoer who has never read the text, who has seen the play only once before and remembers it either roughly or in detail but at least well enough to compare the two productions, is no longer innocent. Any actual performance is the site of convergent, but not necessarily congruent, interpretations. Like directors, actors, and critics, informed playgoers are readers who work from the text to the performance in a process of interpretation based on their reading(s) of the text and their memories of previous performances—and, of course, other memories of the sort studied by psychoanalysts, which I pass over as unnecessary to this critique. In Taylor's scheme such literate playgoers pretend innocence by screening out those operations of reading that would distort or destroy their ability to respond to the moment-by-moment unfolding of the textual manifold: "We want both the impartiality of innocence and the subtlety of experiences in our responses" (12).

This, however, raises a question about the way Taylor formulates the conditions governing the playgoer's ability to respond. Does Taylor's appeal to the laws of perceptual psychology and the principle of economy apply in the same manner to the innocent playgoer and to the informed playgoer who only pretends to be innocent? The informed playgoer may be aware of the parallels and juxtapositions by which the critic is obsessed and may remember the text well enough to pick up repetitions or variations separated by a relatively long interval of performance time.

Consider, for example, the following passage, in which Taylor states that

> a spectator's reaction to Caesar's "I am constant as the Northern star" speech [3.1.58–73] will . . . depend on whether he or she juxtaposes it with Caesar's vacillation in II.ii. . . . The reader juxtaposes two passages as though they were coexistent, and deduces that one undermines the other; but the spectator juxtaposes a present moment with a past one, and as likely as not infers development rather than contradiction. Caesar vacillated then; he is constant now. (148–49)

If the informed playgoer in this situation is reader as well as spectator, his or her inference is not simply the product of perceptual constraints. A context of presuppositions produces the inference, which results from a reinterpretation that is influenced perhaps by a particular production but not, certainly, by the laws of psychology. And of course it is arbitrary to assume that the reader deduces contradiction from coexistence—some readers may and some may not—or that no spectators will infer contradiction rather than development.

Taylor posits an innocent reader whose interpretation is constrained by the laws of graphic inscription and who cannot imagine the constraints or conditions of performance. This is as reductive a fiction as that of the innocent playgoer whose subjection to the laws of psychology can be maintained only in a theory that appends as a corollary the fiction of a presuppositionless experience in theater. What this implies is that the informed reader/spectator, in pretending to be innocent, may also pretend to be bound by the laws of perceptual psychology. Since those laws are constituents of a fictional system, that of the innocent playgoer, it is by an interpretive decision that informed playgoers choose to respect those laws, practice selective amnesia, and organize their responses so as to allow their "anachronistic" knowledge of the text genuinely to increase their "immediate pleasure in and appreciation of a moment of the author's play" (169). Thus even when the informed playgoer is actually at the theater, he or she imagines a set of conditions appropriate to playgoing and *imitates* the role of playgoer in conformity with a *virtual* regime of psychological constraints. That is, he or she adopts and behaves in accordance with an interpretation of playgoing. This interpretation may be a convention, a cultural construction, but the point is that the so-called laws of playgoing psychology belong to that convention rather than to the convention called "nature." Any playgoers who are aware of the convention Taylor describes or who learn it from Taylor's description need not go to the theater to practice informed playgoing. They need only imagine themselves there while reading. Thus a hidden thesis lurks behind Taylor's express proposal. He proposes that informed playgoers feign innocence, but according to that thesis they can also feign playgoing. The informed playgoer may therefore be no less a fiction than the innocent playgoer. *Moment by Moment* is fundamentally a study of *reading* that urges the reader to let his or her interpretive strategies be regulated by one hypothesis, the fiction of performance, rather than by another, the fiction of the "whole," simultaneously graspable, reading text. But the informed reader can play these two hypotheses off against each other, working back and forth between anachronistic—or, to use a less pejorative term, *synchronistic*—and diachronistic analysis. As an informed reader, I can easily imagine myself an informed playgoer imagining himself an innocent playgoer.

The theatrical model of stage-centered reading is no more innocent than Taylor's playgoer. It is by no means a reversion to some pre-typographic paradise of Shakespearean or Elizabethan theater. Rather, it is completely the product of its historical circumstances, since it is constructed in specific opposition to New Critical and other armchair models of reading. In addition, Taylor's version of audience-response criticism is influenced by some features of early reader-response criticism, as he himself implies at one point.[5] As a polemical construction its orientation, like that of reader-response criticism, is determined by the approaches from which it distinguishes itself. A statement made by Jonathan Culler during his account of Derrida's theses on writing and logocentrism aptly describes the audience-response project:

> Privileging speech by treating writing as a parasitic and imperfect representation of it is a way of setting aside certain features of language or aspects of its functioning. If distance, absence, misunderstanding, insincerity, and ambiguity are features of writing, then

by distinguishing writing from speech one can construct a model of communication that takes as its norm an ideal associated with speech—where the words bear a meaning and the listener can in principle grasp precisely what the speaker has in mind.[6]

Privileging theater by reducing the text to a script that imperfectly represents live performance and by reducing valid interpretation to the form of reading that most closely approximates or imitates playgoing reveals similar logocentric commitments. In the grammatological perspective that focuses on the citational, conventional, and role-bound character of speech as a discourse of the other (any of several possible kinds of other, not only the unconscious), the norm dictating that certain features of the text should be set aside so that reading can reproduce the immediacy of the playgoer's experience in the presence of performance is based on an illusory distinction and an arbitrary hierarchy.

Role-bound in the preceding paragraph should not be construed according to the moan of Shakespeare's melancholy misanthrope: "All the world's a stage, / And all the men and women merely players." In the fond fullness of his worldly wisdom Jaques is at best privy to but half the truth. The more interesting half, the half that might make him a real rather than a play misanthrope, the half concealed behind his ignorance that he is himself being played, is that all the world's a text and all the men and women merely characters. Can it really be said, Barbara Johnson asks during her critique of J. L. Austin, "that the chairman who opens a discussion or the priest who baptizes a baby or the judge who pronounces a verdict are persons rather than personae? . . . The performative utterance thus automatically fictionalizes its utterer when it makes him the mouthpiece of a conventionalized authority. . . . Behind the fiction of the subject stands the fiction of society."[7] For anyone who maintains, as Johnson and Derrida do against Austin (and Searle), that all discourse is implicitly "nonserious," the explicit nonseriousness of fictional discourse is the reality that has been repressed, exorcised, quarantined from "serious" discourse in order to produce the fiction of the latter's nonfictionality. Proponents of the logocentric ideal validate the seriousness of "authentic" discourse, enhance its effect of reality, by constituting and upholding over against it the parasitic alterity of discourses they mark as merely fictional or nonserious: "it is fictional language, in the traditional characterization, that brings worlds, complete with objects, persons, events, and intentions, into being, while ordinary or serious language is said to be responsible to the world of empirical fact."[8] Derrida, Johnson, and Fish do not deny that there are differences (but differences that are only ascertainable within "a dimension of assessment") between fictional and ordinary language. Rather, their claim is that it is the latter rather than the former whose effects "are particular, secondary, inscribed, and supplementary";[9] the characteristics of nonserious discourse "infect" and structure serious discourse. It is in precisely these terms that the rank order presupposed by the theatrical model of stage-centered reading lends itself to reversal: priority passes from the theatrical to the literary model as soon as we recognize that the latter makes explicit the imaginary and conventional character of audience response that actual playgoing tends to conceal.

PART TWO

IMAGINARY AUDITION IN
RICHARD II

Introduction

If, as I argued in the last chapter, even so aggressively empirical a version of the theatrical model as Taylor's turns out on examination to be fictional, if spectatorship and audition—along with their privileges and constraints—can be imagined while reading, how is this dimension of stage-centered reading to be incorporated into a practice governed by the privileges and constraints of the literary model? The demonstration that follows is an attempt to recuperate standard features of armchair practice while maintaining a fairly strict focus on the drama of theatrical and interlocutory relations. At the beginning of this study I quoted Sigurd Burckhardt's assertion that actors and directors need help from "those who have the time and patience to *read* Shakespeare, down to the minutest detail," and although I know several actors and directors capable of doing that for themselves, the obviousness of the point about time and patience should not deceive us into overlooking its importance: it gestures toward the most notorious privilege or curse of armchair practice, decelerated reading. This demands as much patience, if less time, from the interpreter's readers as it does from the interpreter, and I can only hope that my painfully slow journey through parts of *Richard II* will not wear that patience out. The slowness derives in part from the complex and multidirectional acts of attention that characterize what I have been calling imaginary audition, a practice which—since up to now I have only alluded to it—I shall now pause to describe.

We practice imaginary audition when, in a dialogue between A and B, we imagine the effect of A's speech on B; listening to A with B's ears, we inscribe the results of this audit in the accounts we render of B's language.[1] But we can also do something else, something persistently encouraged by Shakespearean writing,

45

GOSHEN COLLEGE LIBRARY
GOSHEN, INDIANA

and this something is central to the practice, distinguishing it from more casual forms of auditory attention: we listen to B's language with B's ears. We premise that every interlocutory act is partly a soliloquy in which the speaker constitutes himself as the theater audience he shares confidences with or tries to persuade, affect, deceive. As readers we join B, or B joins us, in monitoring his speech acts. This perspective converts B's speech to continuous self-interpretation or -interrogation so that if at one level we posit B as a speech effect, a character constituted by (our interpretation of) his speech, at another level B reproduces this posit by continuously representing and responding to himself as a speech effect. I plan to submit the speech action of Richard and his interlocutors to imaginary audition of this sort, and I think it is clear that such a project must organize the New Critical staples of armchair practice along theatrical and metatheatrical lines. But since *metatheatrical* has meant different things to different people, these lines must be carefully drawn. Part of the task I have set myself in Chapter 4 is to use the exercise in imaginary audition as springboard to a critique of some examples of metatheatrical theory and practice, a critique that will help me distinguish my version of stage-centered reading from others.

I can't pretend that merely by pretending to listen in on a little of Richard's talk in one or two scenes we can understand what is going on in his language. My reading presupposes a more general hypothesis about the protagonist, one that requires at least some account of the larger context of interpretation within which I place the scene. In the next chapter I shall try to provide this account by exploring stretches of interlocutory action located chiefly in the play's opening scene and in the climactic discoronation scene (4.1).

THREE

"Here, Cousin, Seize the Crown"
The Infamous Victories of King Richard II

Give me the crown. Here, cousin, seize the crown.
Here, cousin,
On this side my hand, and on that side thine.
Now is this golden crown like a deep well
That owes two buckets, filling one another,
The emptier ever dancing in the air,
The other down, unseen, and full of water.
That bucket down and full of tears am I,
Drinking my griefs, whilst you mount up on high.
                                        (4.1.181–89)

The tug-of-war over the crown, as Leonard Barkan aptly calls it,[1] has been repeated in much of the critical commentary on *Richard II* produced since Tillyard's study of the history plays. The majority opinion generally follows Richard in assigning the dancing bucket to the strong, silent, pragmatic usurper and the other to the weak, wordy, self-indulgent king. From the beginning, however, more than a few critics have been tugging in the other direction, finding signs of strength in Richard and of weakness in Bolingbroke. My objective in this study is to add another pair of hands to the minority side in the tug-of-war, though I shall pull the interpretation in a direction somewhat different from that of the critics to whom I am most indebted. One aspect of the difference is my belief that the instigator of the misleading majority image of the weak king is Richard himself. He has succeeded in managing the critics almost as successfully as he manages the course of his deposition. The view of himself and his dilemma that he promotes in the above passage is a false view, but it has prevailed with more communities than the one depicted in the Henriad. He lives in critical history as the down bucket. But according to the somewhat weird physics of the image isn't he—as the full bucket—responsible for sending Bolingbroke's bucket up?

I suspect that the principles behind Richard's bucket physics escape him as well as me; he seems more intent on the interpretive tease value of the image, which he manipulates with the same coyness as the crown. "Here, cousin" is an offer from

> plume-pluck'd Richard, who with willing soul
> Adopts thee heir, and his high scepter yields
> To the possession of thy royal hand.
> Ascend his throne, descending now from him . . .
>   (4.1.108–11)

York's attempt at a genealogical pun gives the last figure an interesting skew: it is the throne, not the incumbent, that will be lowered for the successor's convenience—or his downfall—as Richard gathers new imaginary plumage for his final flight. "Seize the crown" retracts the offer and replaces it with a challenge: "usurp, if you dare." So in his figurative bucketry Richard feints toward one interpretation: "The emptier ever dancing in the air" is easy to identify with "the shallow frivolity of Richard, who even at this moment of disaster hunts after literary conceits."[2] But in the next moment he assigns himself to the down bucket. If the figure recalls "the medieval and Elizabethan figure of Fortune's buckets,"[3] Richard's adaptation to the crown he is toying with suggests, first, that the two men are less the servants than the masters of the fortune they mutually constitute, and, second, that although their movements are interdependent ("two buckets, filling one another") the tearful victim is the dominant force in the partnership.

Barkan's witty and imaginative staging of the tug-of-war underscores Richard's dominance:

> Richard is daring his rival to hold on to the crown, and Bolingbroke is forced to recognize and take part in the charade in a vividly physical way. Richard holds on tight, first as an act of physical defiance . . . and second as a means of forcing Bolingbroke to re-enact, in an almost self-parodic fashion, his usurpation.

Bolingbroke begins the episode half-heartedly, as if humoring a madman, but continues the tug-of-war because he too comes to recognize its symbolism; he has been trapped into doing battle for his manhood. Just when the new king's actual strength is about to win out, Richard willingly lets go, making it clear that his imagination has moved to other, more abstract charades. Bolingbroke is left with a victory so childish and (suddenly) unsymbolic that it is worse than a defeat.[4]

This account can serve as an emblematic condensation of the complicit relationship between Richard and Bolingbroke throughout the play. To suggest what motivates their relationship I shall quickly sketch the two psychological themes that seem to me to be central in the portrait of Richard, the first bearing on his own "inward wars," the second on his position in the family romance.

First, the Richard portrayed by Shakespeare dramatizes the same complex mode of cultural and institutional disenchantment—*despair* is a stronger term for it—that Chaucer depicts in his Pardoner; the same interaction between the impulse to aggression against others and the impulse to aggression against oneself that Chaucer represented and Shakespeare would explore further in *King Lear;* a spiraling oscillation between contempt for self and contempt for others. This interaction is inscribed in Richard's rhetoric and politics. It patterns the course of his behavior and the trajectory of his career. It establishes the psychological framework within which his successors in the Henriad are forced to operate. It motivates the perverse project his skillful management of which argues considerable political finesse: to get himself deposed, pick out a likely "heir" to perform that service, reward him with the title of usurper, and leave him with a discredited crown. The first item in this schedule was announced early in the play by Gaunt: "[thou] art possess't now to depose thyself" (2.1.108).[5]

Some elements of this view of Richard are set forth in James Winny's *The Player King.* Winny argues that from the time of the discoronation scene Richard "leaves the impression of a man wilfully bent on destroying himself" and that he "surrenders himself to Bolingbroke as though he wished to ensure his political abasement, hinting broadly at Bolingbroke's larger ambition before there has been any show of an attempt on the crown."[6] Since he doesn't unpack the implication in this statement, that is to say, that Richard is in effect seducing Bolingbroke, his subsequent account of the sources of Bolingbroke's motivation is weakened. But his discerning comments on Richard go far toward establishing the sources of Richard's motivation:

> He moves towards the state of nothingness as towards the satisfaction of a perverse desire. Although he has insisted that his rights and title are inviolable, he is not prepared to undertake the simplest physical measures to defend them. If the stones will not rise against Bolingbroke, and no angelic host fight the King's battles for him, then Richard must contract out of the political system which has refused to substantiate his idea of the king. He retires into a world of private fantasy.   (59)

The final sentence unfortunately becomes the theme Winny leans on in his subsequent analysis of Richard as shallow and frivolous, self-indulgent, obsessed with words and insubstantial fancies, and therefore politically weak.[7] But the remainder of the passage lays the groundwork for a somewhat different reading. It is not "*his* idea of the king" that the political system has refused to substantiate, it is the idea built into the system itself, and Winny argues that Richard accepts that idea: "Because he cannot divorce himself from the idea of kingly magnificence and sanctity, he habitually speaks of himself as an unearthly being whose trivial acts demand respectful attention" (53). I would place this in the past tense: he has already divorced himself from that traditional idea, knowing very well that he has abused and slandered it and that it had no power to prevent him from doing so.

During the play, when he "speaks of himself as an unearthly being" and invokes the assistance of stones and angels, his rhetoric vibrates with a range of parodic and sarcastic tones the bitterness of which strongly suggests that what Winny describes is something Richard once idealistically believed but no longer believes and now contemns himself for having believed, that is, that "he knows himself King by right of due succession and divine will, and is convinced that no earthly power can depose him" (53). The more pressing question for Richard is whether it is by divine will that he has been able to get away with all he has been accused of, and, if so, what this says about the power of that divine will or about his relation to it. Since at several points in the first two acts he cheerfully demonstrates his lawlessness (1.4.42–61, 59–64; 2.1.153–62, 209–10), his appeals to the rhetoric of divinely ordained kingship in acts 3 and 4 can hardly be accepted at face value. There are not enough clues in his language to enable us to determine whether he is defying or slandering God, whether he is trying to prove that God is helpless to stop him or that he legitimizes knavery.[8] But there are many clues that although he may deem himself beyond forgiveness he is interested in punishment and that he is prepared to subject any conviction of invulnerability to earthly powers to a serious test.[9] In Ernst Kantorowicz's political reading of the play Richard becomes "a traitor to his own immortal body politic and to kingship such as it had been to his day," hence he is complicit in the destruction not only of his "body natural" but also of "the indelible character of the king's body politic, god-like or angel-like."[10] My point is that awareness of the betrayal is inscribed in Richard's language, that it is the source of his self-contempt and of his often sarcastic use of Christian rhetoric, and that the story the Henriad tells concerns the debilitating psychological consequences of that awareness.

This sketch of Richard's "inward wars" is already converging on the second of the two themes I mentioned above: his position in the family romance. Most critics would now agree with Richard Wheeler's general thesis that the Henriad centers "on royal inheritance complicated by patricidal motives in relations to actual and symbolic fathers." Wheeler goes on to note, as Winny does, that Richard "collaborates in his own destruction" and that his behavior seems "calculated to bring on his overthrow . . . and to bring punishment upon himself for his guilty actions."[11] But Wheeler fails to draw the connection between the second observation and the first, between the desire for punishment and the problems attending the transmission of phallic power from fathers to sons, especially in a psychic economy afflicted by a notable shortage of mothers and by what I think is a related failure in paternal authority. Of Richard we might say, with Lady Macduff, "fathered he is and fatherless." The ideal relationship which York describes as having existed between Edward III and the Black Prince fails to repeat itself because either Richard did not assume or his dead father did not renounce the phallic patrimony. The same problem affects Richard's relation to the divine Father who authorizes the patriarchal ideology of kingship. This appears in the mocking irony of his setting himself up as Christ, coming down like Phaeton, and playing the role of a Faustus forced to organize and stage-manage his own secular damnation. And it appears throughout the play in the diffuse contempt that adds bite to his language: contempt for the ideology of kingship; contempt for his performance as king—a performance that slandered the ideology and revealed its powerlessness to restrain his abuses; contempt for himself, perhaps in part for having idealistically believed in divinely sanctioned kingship; contempt for those around him who, if they don't actually believe in that idea, continue to invoke it, especially when they want to excuse or justify the inaction that lets him go on slandering it. Since he is unwilling to inflict on himself the punishment he feels he deserves, he maneuvers others into doing the job for him.[12] The advantage of this strategy is that he can blame them while enjoying the savor of his victimage. The disadvantage is that such a strategy can only increase his self-contempt.

The self-contempt is redirected chiefly toward the fathers who refuse to check him: toward Gaunt, York, and God.[13] If we look at or listen to his opening speech, we can already detect the bitter tonal vibrations:

> Old John of Gaunt, time-honored Lancaster,
> Hast thou according to thy oath and band
> Brought hither Henry Herford thy bold son,
> Here to make good the boist'rous late appeal,
> Which then our leisure would not let us hear,
> Against the Duke of Norfolk, Thomas Mowbray?

"This stilted mode of address," Winny remarks, "suggests the addiction to ceremonial form which Richard seems to find natural" (48). Even Stephen Booth, who thinks the sentence "is gratuitously stuffed and . . . threatens (in 'the . . . late appeal, / Which then our leisure would not let us hear') to come loose from any anchorage in specifics," finds an excuse for it: "this is the start of the play, and the royal flourish of names identifies characters for us."[14] But a closer look at the passage will make the stuffing seem less gratuitous.

The chiasmic patterning of name-title-title-name in the first and last lines works to Gaunt's detriment, since the last line lacks the modifiers that so pointedly distress the iambic pattern of the first. The blunt and familiar opening, "Old John of Gaunt," converts its ceremonial successor to elegant variation and edges it with faint sarcasm. By pushing on the tonal difference between personal and ritual address, Richard turns apposition into opposition, makes the second epithet sound like a euphemistic or mystified equivalent of the first. The first epithet signifies place of birth—John from Ghent—and combines with "Old . . . Gaunt" to suggest the limits of the individual life cycle in which age correlates with weakness or impotence. The second epithet encapsulates the contrary view of age, which protectively surrounds it with a gleaming panoply of tradition, heraldic genealogy, inherited authority, and patriarchally transmitted property. "Time-honored," which can modify the title as well as its holder, adumbrates the ideology of "fair sequence and succession" that York later accuses Richard of violating (2.1.199).[15]

Richard's redundant rush of *h*'s—"Hast [with a touch of *haste*] . . . hither Henry Herford . . . Here . . . hear"—makes his formal request more demanding and importunate; but also more derisive, especially when set against the alliterative coupling of "bold" with "boist'rous." "Bold" wavers between "fearless" or "confident" and "presumptuous" or "forward," while the combination of "son" and "boist'rous" tends to diminish Bolingbroke and stress Gaunt's responsibility for his *boy's* good behavior. Finally, the Variorum, Arden, and Pelican editors take "our leisure" to mean "want" or "lack" of leisure, and the line may indeed be translated as "we didn't have leisure to hear the appeal." But the phrase can equally well mean what it says: "we chose not to let official business interrupt our leisure, our play time." This more acerb version is contrastively emphasized by the alliterative patterns and puns through which Richard characterizes the promptness, the obedience, he expects from Gaunt: "We expect you to hop to it when we give an order. We, on the other hand, will attend to these matters when we aren't busy doing something less important."

All this is entirely in keeping with what we know—with what the play shows everyone knows—about Richard's behavior.[16] From the outset he seems bent on irritating his interlocutors. It may well be, as Leonard Dean observes, that "the glib ritualistic style" of which Richard is master makes one feel that "the king and the nobles are reading lines, that their social behavior is play-acting."[17] Formalized speech establishes ground rules that limit the range of possible responses, conspicuously mask "real" feelings and motives beneath sanctioned artificial replacements, and transfer authority from the speakers themselves to their ceremonial roles. Richard's opening line has the peculiar effect of *signifying* such mystification. It implies that "time-honored Lancaster" misstates the reality of "Old John of Gaunt," and this is odd because one would expect the king to take pains to promote the putative reality of the hierarchic order that preserves his authority. Yet with the very words that activate the ritual mode he flouts it by a mockery extending beyond the individuals to ritual speech and action themselves. It is as if he is daring his audience to show respect for the kingship and the rituals of authority even as he demeans them. If we subsequently judge with Dean "that the ceremony is a hypocritical disguise, that it will not cure the disorder which it is momentarily suppressing" (162), I think this owes much to the various ways, narrative as well as rhetorical, in which Richard reduces it to a travesty. His drive toward self-destruction combines in one scenario two ambivalent motives, Shylock's "I stand for judgment" and Portia's "I stand for sacrifice." But if he wants, like Shylock, to be able to say "I am content," he does not turn to the fathers for such satisfaction. He chooses his cousin Bolingbroke as his Pilate, and prepares him to receive and cultivate his own punishment.

It isn't enough to say that from the first speech of the play Richard is bent on getting deposed. He has already begun the process of selecting the "heir" on whom he will confer the dubious title of usurper—dubious inasmuch as Bolingbroke only takes what Richard gives. This scenario is tucked away in several teasing verbal anticipations that enliven Richard's language. It is expressed in the first scene, though in counterfactual form: "Were he my brother, nay my kingdom's heir" (1.1.116). In 4.1, York will announce that Richard actually has adopted Bolingbroke as his heir (109). In 1.3, when Richard commands the Lord Marshall to "depose him [Bolingbroke] in the justice of his cause," "depose" solicits a proleptic reading—as if Richard already sees Bolingbroke crowned and pronounces a curse ("Let him be deposed"), a curse that nevertheless reflects awareness of his own unjust regime. And this implies a second alternative, "Depose *me* in the justice of his cause." [18]

Another anticipation occurs in Richard's leave-taking of Bolingbroke:

> We will descend and fold him in our arms.
> Cousin of Herford, as thy cause is right,
> So be thy fortune in this royal fight!
> Farewell, my blood; which if today thou shed,
> Lament we may, but not revenge thee dead.
> (1.3.54–58)

In the first line I see not only a foreshadowing of the deposition scene but also a condensed visualization of Richard's latent project as it unfolds through the play, here displaced to the physical circumstance of a ceremonial gesture. The rhythm accentuates the *will* to descend. "Fold him in our arms" is a kinesic hyperbole that mimes the desire coupling Richard to Bolingbroke in their dance toward deposition and regicide, and toward the subsequent regime, when the embrace gradually becomes a stranglehold. The odd reference to "royal fight" also has proleptic force, and the last two lines contribute another foreshadowing. Richard's message is that if Bolingbroke loses he will have unjustly shed the "high blood" his royal kinsman shares, but his language also lets the alternate message, "if you kill me," flicker briefly before us. Whatever we impute to Richard at either the intentional or the motivational level, his actions as well as his language *dare* Bolingbroke to assume the usurper's role: "Here, cousin, seize the crown." One such action occurs in 2.1. After expropriating the Lancastrian inheritance and dismissing in one airy couplet York's long, impassioned protest against this move, Richard blithely announces that he is placing the country in his uncle's unsteady hands while he dashes off to Ireland. All this is staged for the benefit of Northumberland and the other peers who are present, as if to invite and incite the uprising which is already in motion and which only (as he seems to expect) awaits "The first departing of the king for Ireland" (290).

One of the more engaging examples of Richard's relish in advancing this strategy while perversely dominating both the theatrical and the political scene occurs in 1.3 after the sentence of exile has been pronounced. Mowbray has just worked up to a stirring exit with his hyperliterate complaint that he will be deprived of the language he is enjoying so much at this moment (154–73). A rhymed couplet flags the approaching climax of his egress as he prepares to leave the air reverberating behind him: "What is thy sentence then but speechless death, / Which robs my tongue from breathing native breath" (172–73). Exit the unjustly victimized hero into terminal silence. Richard will have none of this limelighting. He covers Mowbray's couplet and prevents his exit with a matching pair that puts down the victim's impotent self-pity: "It boots thee not to be compassionate; / After our sentence plaining comes too late." Forced to try again, Mowbray produces a more elevated pair and threatens to commemorate his departure in a more tragic emblem, an icon of gracious submission to the will of the divine king who condemns him to death or hell: "Then thus I turn me from my country's light, / To dwell in solemn shades of endless night." But Richard still refuses to be upstaged. Once again he frustrates Mowbray's departure by commanding a little ritual which both banished nobles are to perform:

> Return again, and take an oath with thee,
> Lay on our royal sword your banish'd hands,
> Swear by the duty that you owe to God—
> Our part therein we banish with yourselves—
> You never shall, so help you truth and God,
> Embrace each other's love in banishment,
> Nor never look upon each other's face,
> Nor never write, regreet, nor reconcile
> This louring tempest of your home-bred hate,

> Nor never by advised purpose meet
> To plot, contrive, or complot any ill
> 'Gainst us, our state, our subjects, or our land.[19]
> (178–90)

This is a premium-grade example of the "frustration of action and frustrating language" over which Stephen Booth so enjoyably frets:

> Mowbray has started to leave the stage. His part in the scene is over. Richard then calls him back; Richard thus does to the scene something like what he does to his sentences. Moreover, Richard causes Mowbray and Bolingbroke to present an on-stage tableau of precisely the action they swear never to take: they join their hands and swear together. . . . The syntax of the speech that promotes the cooperative response also enacts the fusion it prohibits. The first line pertains only to Mowbray. . . . The rest of the speech is addressed to Mowbray and Bolingbroke jointly.
> ("Syntax as Rhetoric," 94–95)

Booth's description increases in force when its comment on Richard's antic theater is extended to the king's political scenario. Richard is careful to give specific instructions about the sorts of things the exiles are not to do. Since at this point nobody expects them to dishonor their professions of mutual enmity by forming an alliance, the speech is gratuitous and carries the weight of an insult. Thus Richard's diligent itemization is not only a display of apprehensiveness; it also seems intended to rankle, as does the order that joins the two together in a symbolic tableau of cooperation. But that intention edgily invites a risk: as Richard lists the sorts of things they might well do if they are willing to overcome their scruples and home-bred hate when abroad, his prohibitions begin to sound like dares or proposals. "Our part therein we banish with yourselves": "In banishing you we absolve you from your duty to us" (Ure's gloss in the Arden edition, 32), which is to say, "You are now free to dissociate us from God." This is a little more than the "vaingloriously magnanimous," "thoughtless," and "self-serving" parenthesis Booth claims it is ("Syntax as Rhetoric," 95). In the context supplied above it adds sharpness to both the taunt and the dare: "If you are dishonorable enough to join forces, no obligation to our part in the divine kingship need stand in the way of your returning to lay banished hands on our royal sword, crown, and body."

Booth applies to Richard his distinction between characters as fictive persons "whom audiences recognize as somehow pleasant or unpleasant" and characters as theatrical commodities "who are actually pleasing or displeasing to an audience." Richard, Booth argues, "has frustrated both the action and the audience" in the first act and has become "a source of theatrical irritation to the audience *as* audience" (88). This is "not the Richard who efficiently misuses his power" in 2.1, but "the ineffectual Richard . . . who has power and wastes it" (95) and whose inefficient syntax makes him hard to listen to. When Richard returns from Ireland as the political underdog and victim in 3.2 he has, according to Booth, cleaned up his syntactical act and, "as many commentators have noticed, audiences now like him better; we recognize him as the contemptible human being he always was, but we no longer find him 'hard to take.'" His sentences now "*deliver*; they deliver the same old stuff, but they bring it right up to the door of understanding" (96–97).

I would like once again to link these perceptions more closely to the motivational drama I have been describing. If Richard arouses the audience's antipathy in the first act this provides a theatrical intensifier or reflector of his attempt to mobilize the aggressivity diffusely circulating throughout the court community and to focus it on himself. When he first calls Mowbray and Bolingbroke "to our presence" his words momentarily suggest that the opposing knights will confront him rather than each other:

> face to face,
> And frowning brow to brow, ourselves will hear
> The accuser and the accused freely speak.
> (1.1.15–17)

This passing image is reinstated and stabilized when Richard commands them to join hands on the royal sword. And when he returns from Ireland his success in attracting aggression enables him to step comfortably into the victim's role he has solicited. "From that point until the last seconds of his life . . . Richard is gloriously, self-indulgently, volubly, extravagantly, ineffectual" (Booth, "Syntax as Rhetoric," 96) and, in terms of his own perverse political project, effective.

My view of this scenario develops an idea long ago suggested by Dover Wilson and Tillyard, the idea that although Bolingbroke "acts forcibly he appears to be borne upward by a power beyond his volition," grows increasingly bewildered, "has no steady policy and . . . is the servant of fortune." [20] The power that bears him up is Richard. To be more precise, it is the vector sum of the close collaboration between Richard and Bolingbroke as each, by his acts, helps progressively to sharpen and define motives in the other that appear initially to have been vague, hesitant, indecisive, or not fully articulated. Bolingbroke's words and actions in the early scenes do not reveal any clear plan. He seems diffusely aggressive, ready for anything but not certain as to what precise course he will take. He jumps abruptly forward with imperious gestures, then nervously backtracks into deferential postures. Richard helps him convert a vacillating tendency toward usurpation into a definite project. As A. R. Humphreys justly observes, "Richard's despairing haste to yield power virtually thrust[s] the crown into Bolingbroke's hands." [21] But in doing this Richard also thrusts a curse into Bolingbroke's hands. The succession of kings in the Henriad is a genealogy of guilt which, seeded in Richard's own self-division, transmits itself with increasing virulence. The virulence testifies to the abiding power of the murdered king, a power seriously underestimated by the canonical view of Richard as a weak and politically inept ruler who victimized, if anyone, only himself. This view is hard to uphold in the face of Richard's performance in the discoronation scene, to which I now return after noting that the essence of his performance is encapsulated in his wicked little game of "Here, cousin, seize the crown": "Here, cousin" offers a gift and dangles the bait, while "seize the crown" retracts the offer, publishes the act as a usurpation, and transfers both blame and guilt along with the crown to the usurper.

"It is too simple," Lois Potter argues, "to treat the deposition scene as a triumph of silent, powerful Bolingbroke over verbose, weak Richard. Language *is* a source of power in the play, even though there is also awareness of its inadequacy." My view of this scene is in some respects very close to Potter's and owes much to her concise demonstration that what Richard "wins is not simply a moral victory; by making it clear that he is not willing to resign the crown and still considers himself the rightful king, he has opened the way for just such a conspiracy as we see taking shape at the end of the scene." He has, that is, ironically proved the power of the king's language, first, by deposing himself (since "only a king can judge a king"), and, second, by encouraging sedition against the next regime. Potter emphasizes Richard's mastery of tight-corner politics: "it is he who must depose himself, yet the very fact that he is in this humiliating position is also a proof of his kingship which nothing can eradicate," and he makes the most of his predicament.[22]

Potter doesn't come to grips with the other side of this emphasis, however: Richard uses his kingship to prove and make the most of his humiliating position. Nor does she explain how or why he got into this position. At one point she acknowledges that it may be "possible to argue that his anticipation of Bolingbroke's intentions makes Richard an accomplice in his own destruction," but she goes on to assume what has to be proved, rejecting this possibility out of hand because it "seems to me too 'psychological' an approach to the plays" (37). My defense of the possibility rests on a somewhat scrambled version of Potter's postulate about language, which is that for Richard the performative power of his language displays and derives from its strategic inadequacy to express what "lies all within," that his enjoyment of the power displays and derives from his own inadequacy, and that his successful deployment of its power proves and derives from the inadequacy of everyone else. This formulation is in essential agreement with a thesis Potter nicely states but doesn't fully explore: that although "elaborate language is used as a substitute for action and, to that extent, . . . may be a sign of weakness in those who speak it, it is itself extremely powerful" (33)—precisely because, I hasten to add, it is a sign of weakness.

Accent on the performative power of language suggests that we might look for help from speech-act theory, and in fact one of the more interesting approaches to Richard's language has been attempted from that perspective by Joseph Porter.[23] In a brief but telling revision of the view that Richard is "a poet figure," Porter argues that his poetic character lies less in his "arialike effusions" than in his tendency to think and speak "of language as a material from which to construct literary objects" (34–35). Often "he talks of speech virtually as the projection of an object by breath"; his phrase "frozen admonition" at 2.1.117 both instantiates and illustrates the way "verbal *acts*" congeal into "verbal *objects*" when they leave the mouth (36). Furthermore, he "thinks of himself not only as a constructor" of such objects "but also as the object constructed" (34–35), and constructed as the hero not merely of his own lyric poems but, on a larger scale, of his inventions in narrative genres: he speaks of his life and conceives of "his own actions as if they stood outside time like events in a story" (33–34). Since his "language is a medium for constructing expressions rather than for expressing," his objectified self-representation "is tied to the self even less than 'external manners [of lament],'" and consequently the words that *express* the self must falsify it. "From time to time . . . he talks as if there were adequate words of the self which, by his odd logic, in order to be authentic must not be uttered" (37).

I find these comments both stimulating and frustrating. Stimulating, because they suggest important connections between what Porter calls Shakespeare's "local dramaturgy" and the themes of the psychopolitical discourse I have been exploring; frustrating, because the limited resources and objectives of speech-act theory prevent Porter from taking advantage of the connections. He seeks instead a more persuasive way to account for Richard's powerlessness in terms of his poetic approach to speech acts: Richard's failure lies in his inability or refusal "to admit time into the scope of his attention." Because he is a "poet," he "conceives of language as a material in which to construct timeless objects . . . rather than a medium in which acts are performed" (49–50). As Porter sees it, "the overall action of the play is the decline and fall" of Richard's speech, his "conception of language," his "linguistic world" (42–43). Thus *Richard II* is reduced to a play about speech-act theory. Richard misfires because his tendency to use language poetically derives from an infelicitous theory of speech acts. His hapless "exercitives" are discharged into a nonserious realm of timeless fictions. "Both the soliloquylike nature of his 'dialogue' and its ceremonial explicitness manifest an avoidance of using language for interaction and they isolate him from his interlocutors so that his speech cannot have direct consequences" (50).

Even this thesis, however, contains generative insights that can be developed by redirecting it from Richard's powerlessness *tout court* to his perverse enjoyment in the representation of powerlessness and to the power he gains over Bolingbroke by his deployment of that representation. What the "direct consequences" of his speech are we have already seen, and their relation to his penchant for self-construction through inauthentic utterance deserves more attention than Porter devotes to it. Nicholas Brooke has argued that the ritualism and ceremonial rhetoric of the play support "a view of the divine order which is . . . seen as splendid, but none the less making demands of men which cannot be fulfilled"; one symptom of this problem is that "the more we are allowed to see Richard's deficiencies as a man, the more powerfully his glory is imagined." [24] To give Brooke's insight a more perverse psychological bounce we can say that the more Richard tastes his deficiencies, the more powerfully he sends up the rhetoric of glory. His language conveys the suspicion that humans are worthless apart from the roles they assume or receive in the ritual order. If what he deems "authentic" about his "self" is its inauthenticity, then it follows that the ritual order and its public roles are necessarily hypocritical: every *ex*pression of "emotion," every gesture that sustains a role before an audience, falsifies or fictionalizes whatever impulse gave rise to it.

From the moment of his entry in 4.1 Richard seems to try both to prove his inauthenticity to himself and to escape from it by ascending the "heaven of invention" so that he may ensconce himself in fictions that will in time take on the ring of truth. His parade of sorrows has the positive function of creating and preserving a particular image of himself and bequeathing it to his stage audience. As Lois Potter perceptively demonstrates, the man of sorrows makes no bones about his duplicity, continuing his practice "of giving with one hand and taking away with the other" ("Antic Disposition," 38). My point about this is not only that the "giving" is a seduction and a trap but also that the practice is Richard's way of rubbing salt into his own sinfulness as well as the usurper's. After the tug-of-war and the improvised rite in which he formally deposes himself, he refuses to read out the articles that list the "grievous crimes / Committed by your person and your followers / Against the state and profit of this land" (4.1.223–25). Why, he asks Northumberland, must he "ravel out / My weav'd-up follies?" Wouldn't it shame Northumberland to read his offenses before "so fair a troop," especially since they include "the deposing of a king," "a blot, damn'd in the book of heaven" (230–36)? Everyone seems to assume and no one, including Richard, seems to deny that his regime as a whole constituted a betrayal of trust, so that if he is or believes himself to be the "deputy of the Lord" it follows that his offenses are written in the same book. Hence it is hilariously airy of him not only to reduce the "grievous crimes" he acknowledges to mere follies but also to hold them up as a tapestry and claim that the bad taste of reciting them before a troop of usurpers would damage the artwork. And there is more in this move than airiness. By refusing to read the articles he maintains the focus on the usurpers' crime even as he insists on undoing himself. His sin, as he carefully formulates it throughout the scene, derives not from the "grievous crimes" of his regime (those follies have passed from the artist to his work) but only from the present act of self-deposition. He plies this formulation with a kind of bitter delight in its illogicality—the illogicality of "Here, cousin, seize the crown" with which he bullies poor Bolingbroke, who is to be stigmatized as a usurper yet denied the manly pleasure of claiming that he won the throne without Richard's help.

Richard goes on to compound the outrage by staging himself as Christ betrayed by Judases and victimized by Pilates who, although they wash their hands and show "an outward pity," have "deliver'd me to my sour cross, / And water cannot wash away your sin" (241–42). Immediately after this he joins them, finding himself "a traitor with the rest" for consenting to be deposed—another confessional misdirection that, like the refusal to read the articles, shifts attention from the treasonous regime to the treasonous act that concludes it. Implicit in this crossover is his acceptance of a share in the "heinous article" of deposition he imputes to Northumberland. So it seems appropriate for him to blame his refusal on the water he adds to Pilate's futile purification—"Mine eyes are full of tears, I cannot see" (244)—and then a little later, resuming the victim's pose, to wish not for absolution but for dissolution. The wish unrolls in hyperboles that savor both the desire to be purged of himself and the futility of the desire: he is

> no man's lord. I have no name, no title,
> No, not that name was given me at the font,
> But 'tis usurp't. Alack the heavy day,
> That I have worn so many winters out,
> And know not now what name to call myself!
> O that I were a mockery king of snow,
> Standing before the sun of Bolingbroke,
> To melt myself away in water-drops!
> (255–62)

The final line recalls the cry uttered by Doctor Faustus just before being carried off to Hell: "O soul, be changed into small water-drops / And fall into the ocean, ne'er be found." This is the last of Faustus's five hysterical fantasies of escape from eternal damnation, and it is the most powerful not only because it is a poignant parody of absolution but also because its focus on the dissolution of the soul is associated with the wish to deny his identity, "Curs'd be the parents that engender'd me," a denial he immediately negates in "No Faustus, curse thyself." This cluster of motifs, repeated along with other Marlovian echoes in the deposition scene, composes into an allusive network that challenges one of the standard interpretations of the scene. Anne Righter Barton, for example, argues that at this point the down bucket hits bottom: Richard "has no position, virtually no existence. He is a kind of nothing." Robert Ornstein and James Calderwood concur: "Like the dying Faustus . . . Richard is tormented by a realization of loss and emptiness"; in this moment Shakespeare dramatizes "an ultimate loss of name and a consequent dissolution of personal identity and meaning."[25] But such a view of poor Richard ignores his own enthusiastic contribution to it. Poor Richard is an effect of *his* language, not merely of Shakespeare's.

What *Doctor Faustus* adds to this effect may best be focused by mediating it through Stephen Greenblatt's thesis that the repetitive pattern of the Marlovian hero's "willful courting of disaster" is ironically motivated by his "will to self-fashioning. Marlowe's heroes struggle to invent themselves; they stand, in Coriolanus' phrase, 'As if a man were author of himself / And knew no other kin.'" Thus "we never see and scarcely even hear of the hero's parents." The parents Faustus curses were "base of stock," but Marlowe's heroes also fashion themselves "in self-conscious opposition" to absolute authority and to "the structure of sacramental and blood relations that normally determine identity in this period."[26] These observations are as applicable to Richard as they are to Faustus. In fact they are more applicable, because if both Faustus's spiritual melodrama and the megaphonics of Marlovian theater are heard in the echo chamber of *Richard II*, they are present as a model to be corrected or repudiated, and the similarities between the heroes serve to draw attention to their differences.[27]

Faustus's twenty-four-year spree concludes in despair and is followed by eternal pain, but most of the play withdraws into the pastoral of magical pranks. The repetitive impulse to self-cancellation inscribed in Richard's pattern of self-deposition is motivated from the beginning by a desperate bitterness—Richard's spree is virtually over when the play begins. The savor of speech acts that court destruction *and* damnation imparts to his language an astringency lacking in Faustus's. In the case of *Doctor Faustus* it is possible to argue that Faustus's pact with the devil articulates the structure of his despair, and Greenblatt describes his signing the deed with Christ's dying words as "the uncanny expression of a perverse, despairing faith, . . . the culmination of Faustus's fantasies of making an end, and hence a suicide that demonically parodies Christ's self-sacrifice" (214). However, neither the organization of the play nor its language during the long parade of episodic pastimes keeps this theme before us—unless, that is, we take the parade as Marlowe's picture of what Richard, in 3.2, calls the "sweet way . . . to despair." But the self-slandering undertone of Richard's rhetoric has no parallel in *Doctor Faustus.*

Shakespeare's citational use of *Doctor Faustus* is more than a revision. It is a parodistic representation both of Faustus's spiritual melodrama as conceived by Marlowe and of Marlowe's own rhetorical theatricality. The two are compacted into a single effect and displaced to Richard. That is, insofar as Faustus's morality play and Marlowe's, Faustus's bombastic grandeur and Marlowe's, are glimpsed in *Richard II*, they are present as an identity, a single citational system which is localized in Richard rather than in the play as a whole. And the system is localized not at the surface of his discourse, which—with one exception—is always public and aimed at an audience, but in the subtext that Richard aims at himself as he works and plays on his own feelings behind the ritualized screen of speech that works and plays on the feelings of his interlocutors. His Faustian subtext not only differs from its model, it subverts it, for Faustus wants to defer or evade the torments of the fiend while Richard's language vertiginously tempts them.

Doctor Faustus is apolitical, indeed antipolitical, insofar as its topical satire is relegated to episodes in the chronicle of the hero's personal damnation. But Richard's desire to reinvent himself—as Christ, as Judas, as the master of his own deposition and the victim of usurpation—is not played out for his benefit alone. It has a psychopolitical purpose. To borrow Greenblatt's useful concept, it is a continuous act of *improvisation* whereby he transforms his fictional self-fashioning into Bolingbroke's reality (*Renaissance Self-Fashioning*, 227–29). If Richard is to be damned, he will take Bolingbroke with him and will leave his malediction on future regimes.

Thus to reduce him to Poor Richard, the down bucket, is to place oneself in Bolingbroke's shoes and be seduced by the sentimentalized self-projection that is parodied by the energy and cunning of his verse. For consider lines 255–62 more closely. The alliterative jingling of the last five lines points up the chief effect of the passage: relish in finding and developing another conceit with which to stuff the victim's plight into his auditor's ears. "Alack . . . / That I have worn so many winters out" is so splendidly evasive as to target the years of misrule it pretends to wash away: Richard knows his auditors know how he wore out those winters, as well as their fellow springs and summers. His negations acknowledge the title, name, and lordship to which his crimes against the state adhere. Even the wish to be dissolved is voiced aggressively. Barton suggests that Richard reaches the nadir when the sun image is "transferred to Bolingbroke, now Henry IV," at line 261, and that from this point on Richard is relentlessly pursued by "the image of the actor," symbol "of what is unsubstantial and unreal" (*Shakespeare*, 124). But apart from the fact that it is Richard who transfers the image, a glance at the difference between his final phrase and its Faustian predecessor makes it clear that he denies the sun full credit for the snow king's liquefaction. He does not say, for example, "To melt away into small water-drops." He says he will *stand* before the sun and *melt himself away*. "With mine own tears I wash away my balm" (4.1.207).

The image of the actor does not pursue Richard as relentlessly as he pursues it, especially the image of an actor in the Marlovian mode. The pattern of revisionary allusion to *Doctor Faustus* continues at line 270, where Richard's performance of spiritual melodrama is again deepened by contrast to the precursor it evokes. It is occasioned by the fourth of Northumberland's nervously repeated attempts to legitimize the deposition by having Richard recite his crimes against the state. "Read o'er this paper while the glass doth come," he urges Richard, and the jitteriness Richard's histrionics arouses in him is wonderfully condensed in that little word *o'er*, which encourages by understating the task: "Don't make too much of it; just run through it quickly; confess while you wait." Richard therefore obliges with a Faustian bellow that maximizes the import of the request: "Fiend, thou torments me ere I come to hell." This embarrasses Bolingbroke and spotlights Northumberland's poor taste and timing: since Richard has already, and by his own effort, earned his place in hell, it is gratuitous as well as presumptuous of Northumberland to usurp the devil's function. Northumberland replaces the Bad Angel in *Doctor Faustus*, at whose disclosure of the "vast perpetual torture-house" Faustus exclaims, "O, I have seen enough to torture me." Richard's echo mocks itself, in part because his utterance acknowledges his crimes and sins even as he inflates—or reduces—Northumberland to one of the powers of darkness that control his fate. It is also self-mocking for another reason, which is suggested by the Bad Angel's response to Faustus: "Nay, thou must feel them, taste the smart of all— / He that loves pleasure must for pleasure fall." Richard may be imagined to say this to himself; feeling the torments and tasting the smart is his peculiar pleasure. And as his own Bad Angel he pursues another quarry, the soul of Bolingbroke.

This quest continues in the mirror episode, where the demand for a looking glass is a taunting response to Northumberland's fuss over having Richard read the articles. Richard proposes an alternative:

> I'll read enough
> When I do see the very book indeed
> Where all my sins are writ, and that's myself.
> (273–75)

Declining to "read" the sins by which he has wounded the body politic, he turns instead to survey those inscribed on the reflected surface of the body natural. And what does he find?

> No deeper wrinkles yet? hath sorrow struck
> So many blows upon this face of mine
> And made no deeper wounds? O flatt'ring glass,
> Like to my followers in prosperity,
> Thou dost beguile me. Was this face the face
> That every day under his household roof
> Did keep ten thousand men? Was this the face
> That like the sun did make beholders wink?
> Is this the face which fac'd so many follies,
> That was at last out-fac'd by Bolingbroke?
> A brittle glory shineth in this face;
> As brittle as the glory is the face,
> For there it is, crack'd in an hundred shivers.
> (277–89)

What he finds is not that the mirror mirrors the face but that the face mirrors the mirror. It is the face, not its image, that beguiles him. This false face passes in the third sentence into the intact smoothness of the flattering glass and thence into the flatterers, the ten thousand kept and winking men who had beguiled him with an equally false reflection of the royal "self" he desired—beguiled him as Mephistophilis had beguiled Faustus with the image of Helen. In Marlowe's play the occasion of Helen's appearance is Faustus's desperate request for a final pleasure to stave off the impulse to repent; he would ease the way to Hell with "sweet embraces" that "extinguish clear / Those thoughts that do dissuade me from my vow" to Lucifer. Richard's requesting and smashing the mirror reverberates a Faustian reconfirmation of the will to undo himself; the "hundred shivers" are indeed shivers as well as slivers. Faustus fixes on the politically destructive force of Helen's beauty and Richard reads a similar power in the image that beguiles him: his phrase, "under his household roof," evokes a thought of Ilium's "topless towers" (where "topless" condenses "cloud-capped" and "toppled").[28]

In Richard's little Marlovian tragedy the followers who earned their keep with shows of service, compliance, and sunstruck awe were his tempters and (mis)leaders; *follower* denotes a familiar spirit or devil as well as a pursuer. The face the mirror shows is itself the reflection of their folly in thus beguiling such a ruler as he knows himself to be. "So many follies" has a summary ring to it but it is influenced by "ten thousand men" and must include their tendency to shut their eyes to "the very book" as well as his ability to make them do so. His folly was to lend his countenance to their follies, to reflect, adorn, and *illustrate* them in the brittle glory of his glassy face.

This is Richard's tart response to Northumberland, and it blithely continues the effrontery he has been summing up: instead of reciting the text that lists his crimes, he plays the histrionic fool and, like Pilate, shows "an outward pity"—but pity for himself beguiled by fair-weather followers and victim of his own prodigal generosity and splendor. Reading his mirrored face as the mirror of that folly, as the image of an image, flaunts his refusal to open up "the very book." Yet at the same time it displays the sins inscribed therein. For perhaps Richard remembers as well as we do the sentence from Gaunt's diatribe that "ten thousand men" echoes:

A thousand flatterers sit within thy crown,
Whose compass is no bigger than thy head,
And yet, incaged in so small a verge,
The waste is no whit lesser than thy land.
                                        (2.1.100–103)

The tenfold increase is more than an acknowledgment of Gaunt's rebuke; it is a boast. But the feeling behind the boast is darkened by another echo with which these two passages are linked:

within the hollow crown
That rounds the mortal temples of a king
Keeps Death his court, and there the antic sits,
Scoffing his state and grinning at his pomp,
Allowing him a breath, a little scene,
To monarchize, be fear'd, and kill with looks . . .
                                        (3.2.160–65)

The verbal pleasure informing all his cameos of despair is proof rather than disproof of Richard's self-despite. Every impulse toward confession or self-exposure finds utterance only in rhetorical self-parody that "contemns it[s] origin," to borrow Albany's phrase.

The conspicuous artificiality and copiousness of Richard's verse convey this effect. They signify the speaker's delight in the words and images through which he continually effaces and reinvents himself. They also signify his disbelief in them. Delight *in* disbelief figures the *curiositas* of his despair. But delight *and* disbelief converge in a demonic conjunction that produces the peculiar power his language solicits: power "whose quintessential sign is the ability to impose one's fictions upon the world; the more outrageous the fiction, the more impressive the manifestation of power." This is Greenblatt's paraphrase of one part of Thomas More's answer to the question, "Why should men submit to fantasies that will not nourish or sustain them?"; they submit because even if no one "is deceived by the charade . . . everyone is forced"—like Bolingbroke—"either to participate in it or to watch it silently." The other part of More's answer is that his "is a world in which everyone is profoundly committed to upholding conventions in which no one believes; somehow belief has ceased to be necessary" because of the anxiety that beneath "the layer of theatrical delusion" there may be "nothing at all" (*Renaissance Self-Fashioning*, 13–14). Greenblatt accepts and develops More's first insight, arguing that one of the "supreme pleasures" of European rulers of this period was "to enforce the acceptance of fictions that are known to be fictions" (141). Both insights profoundly illuminate *Richard II* if certain reservations are attached. For one thing, radical skepticism is not the bottom line in the Henriad, since all three kings are haunted by a suspicion that the sacramental order which has been violated is real; for them, as for Hamlet, "the dread of something after death . . . puzzles the will," and in varied, subtle, but equally powerful ways conscience makes cowards of them all. From this follows a second and more important reservation, which is that although Richard may try to "enforce the acceptance of fictions" that *he* knows to be fictions, the quintessential sign of his power will be his successor's delusion that they are real. To say that "the face which fac'd so many follies, / . . . was at last out-fac'd by Bolingbroke" is to suggest that Bolingbroke will now replace him by facing Richard's follies. Bolingbroke will be his follower in prosperity: the fiend that pursues him and the successor who, countenancing Richard's interpretation of himself, will inherit the brittleness of his glory and follow him to hell.

The direction this project takes is suggested by the concluding lines of the mirror episode:

> Mark, silent king, the moral of this sport—
> How soon my sorrow hath destroy'd my face.
> *Bol.*   The shadow of your sorrow hath destroy'd
> The shadow of your face.
> *Rich.*   Say that again.
> The shadow of my sorrow? ha! let's see—
> 'Tis very true, my grief lies all within,
> And these external manners of lament
> Are merely shadows to the unseen grief
> That swells with silence in the tortur'd soul.
> There lies the substance.   (290–99)

Superficially, Richard's reply undoes itself because it is another external manner of lament.[29] As shadows or players of his unseen grief, his words fall short in that their rhetorical embodiment falsifies it. For he appears to be harping on his victimization and loss of power at the hands of others, while clearly, in a flaunt that belies his words, enjoying his theatrical control over Bolingbroke. Concealed under the sound and shadow of lament, his "tortur'd soul" silently continues to direct the project, which finds deferred expression—and fruition—only in the words of the heir whom he, in God's name, has appointed to "breed revengement and a scourge for me" and has "mark'd / For the hot vengeance and the rod of heaven, / To punish my mistreadings" (*1 Henry IV*, 3.2.7–11). "There lies the substance" that swells beneath the lying shadows that veil "the very book indeed / Where all my sins are writ." It may be arbitrary to read "lies" as a pun and then to ascribe it to the speaker as his pun, but this move is consonant with the argument I have been developing: it indicates Richard's knowing and mocking reference to the way he continues to parade his mistreadings for his own perverse delectation, continues also to tease Bolingbroke with coded gestures toward self-exposure which, like the crown, he half offers and half withholds.

Those lies aspire to the condition of a truth whose general drift has been remarked by Brooke: Richard's guilt "is reflected on Bolingbroke, who, seated on his throne, is another 'mirror' of Richard's predicament" and whose "silent figure adds to its emblematic connotations that of 'silence in the tortured soul'. Their guilts reflect each other" (*Shakespeare's Early Tragedies*, 132). This way of putting it, however, obscures Richard's share in the insight since it is, after all, *his* interpretation (not merely Shakespeare's) of the mirror-smashing. And it dulls the proleptic force of the reflected moral. The moral is at first political: "My sorrow will soon become yours when you assume the brittle glory of the royal face." But after Bolingbroke dismisses the gesture as a stagy tantrum Richard counters with a play on "shadow" that drives the moral deeper: "My tantrum emblematically acts out and foreshadows the unseen grief that will swell with silence in *your* tortured soul until it destroys *your* face."[30] Richard's next words allow a glimpse of this moral:

> And I thank thee, king,
> For thy great bounty, that not only giv'st
> Me cause to wail, but teaches me the way
> How to lament the cause.
>
> (299–302)

"You are the cause of my wailing, and you teach me how to lament *for* that cause," that is, "lament for you as well as for myself." Bolingbroke's may be a "shrewd retort" (Brooke, *Shakespeare's Early Tragedies*, 133) but it offers a clue to the power, the "mortal touch," that will make him suffer: the power of the actor's stagy grief to produce an illusion—the Christlike victim and his lamentable fall—whose shadow deepens until at the end of his life Bolingbroke acknowledges "the soil of the achievement": "For all my reign hath been but as a scene / Acting that argument" (*2 Henry IV*, 4.5.189, 197–98).[31]

To summarize this account of 4.1: Richard's performance of the discoronation rite and its sequel is a work of genius at both the political and the psychological level. On the one hand he formally reenacts the self-deposition he has helped bring about, thereby publicly demonstrating his active relinquishment of the crown. On the other hand he forces Bolingbroke to reenact his usurpation, thereby publicly dramatizing the illegal seizure. The transfer of power is framed as a transfer of guilt and, following Bolingbroke's instruction, Richard projects his shadow across his successor's reign by marking him with the bequest which Bolingbroke will later try in vain to displace to Exton: "The guilt of conscience take thou for thy labor" (5.6.41). Bolingbroke will become the double, the shadow, the spiritual son and scapegoat who carries off Richard's guilt and self-affright. Yet he remains oblivious to Richard's share in the action and seems quickly to forget the charges that originally motivated the appeal he directed at Richard through Mowbray: the murder of Gloucester and "all the treasons for these eighteen years / Complotted and contrived in this land" (1.1.95–96). Any partially mitigating circumstances melt away as the "brittle glory" shining from Richard's image "darts his light" ever deeper into Bolingbroke's conscience.

FOUR

Imaginary Audition and Metatheater
Richard II, 3.2 (I)

The canonical view of Richard as a weak king prevails even among those commentators—increasingly numerous in recent decades—who insist that Richard is effective in theatrical terms, so much so that he upstages Bolingbroke throughout the play. Such a distinction between political and theatrical effectiveness is in my opinion a chimera. It is produced in part by a failure to take seriously the *politics* of speech acts—the power relations that interlocutory competition not only manifests but also constitutes—and in part by a failure to connect Richard's preeminence in this performative skill with the resonance of spiritual despair that edges his language, a sharp and wicked resonance that testifies to the *curiositas* theologians and psychologists have always associated with despair. Richard's *curiositas* is probing and experimental, and the language that expresses it delights in its own power even as it gives off vibrations of anger and contempt. If we listen with Richard's ears not only to his speech but also to the messages his interlocutors seem by their responses to receive, we may come to suspect that some of the anger and contempt is directed toward them for their inability to hear the anger and contempt he directs toward himself, and this in spite of the fact that he takes a kind of voyeuristic pleasure in encouraging their obtuseness by maintaining the gap between what he hears himself say and what they hear him say. To pick out this interlocutory play, fix one's attention on it, and interpret it is to practice imaginary audition.

It will clarify my own position if I begin by briefly identifying one view of Richard I strenuously oppose, a view whose major thesis is the product of a certain kind of practice which the readings that follow are intended to challenge. This is the view that Richard's "keen sense of theatrical effect" is in the service of a dominantly narcissistic, lyrical, and estheticizing sensibility: "Poet, actor, dreamer, passive spectator—all these qualities unavoidably lead him to revel in imagery whenever he speaks. Instead of deciding, he interprets the situation by means of elaborate similes; instead of turning to action, he prefers to reflect upon his own state." [1] This view is the logical consequence of a practice that treats Richard's major speeches in isolation as if they were soliloquies, meditations uttered primarily for his own benefit—an effect produced by screening out the rhetorical contexts that clearly give them the value of *performances* directed at his auditors as well as at himself. My task in exploring 3.2 will thus be to accentuate the context of performance and audition, and I think it important to reiterate that for me this context— what Joseph Porter calls "the drama of speech acts"—is not merely the scene of theater but also the scene of politics. The political drama of the play is most forcefully expressed in the patterns of verbal thrust, parry, and riposte that shape its "local dramaturgy" (Porter, *The Drama of Speech Acts*, 37). And I submit that Richard is the play's preeminent politician, both in these terms and in the wider context of the strange scenario I described above.

Richard's politics are primarily interlocutory, by which I mean that his speech focuses those conflicts of power and struggles for authority that dominate the dialogue. It is a politics of speech acts, and it demands a finely tuned but flexible deployment of the auditory imagination. Like the eyes of tennis watchers, readers must follow with their "ears" the movement of meaning back and forth from speaker to auditor, from one auditor to another, from auditor to speaker, and—most important—from speaker to himself. The complexity of audition demanded by Shakespeare's major speakers owes much to the sense that even in their most formal and public utterances they seem often to be listening to and acting on themselves. In *Shakespeare's Poetic Styles* John Baxter mentions this reflexive phenomenon in passing and cites the comment Erich Auerbach makes on it in his essay on

Montaigne. Of Montaigne's "Let us only listen [to ourselves]: we tell ourselves all we most need," Auerbach writes that "the method of listening (*escoutons y*) can be applied with any degree of accuracy only to the experimenter's own person; it is in the last analysis a method of self-auscultation, of the observation of one's own inner movement." [2]

Baxter adverts to this passage only to criticize Shakespeare's representation of the method in *Richard II* as responsible for the solipsism and libertinism that flaw the play and make it fall "short of the reality of tragic vision" (125–27). In the present study I shall try to demonstrate the contrary thesis: the textual traces of Richard's self-auscultation account for what I take to be the success and power of the play. Discursive self-reference is one of the play's most prominent activities, and Emile Benveniste's comments on its function in Freudian analysis may serve as a preface to the kind of interpretation I shall undertake in the discussion that follows:

> All through Freudian analysis it can be seen that the subject makes use of the act of speech and discourse in order to "represent himself" to himself as he wishes to see himself and as he calls upon the "other" to observe him. His discourse is . . . a sometimes vehement solicitation of the other through the discourse in which he figures himself desperately, and an often mendacious recourse to the other in order to individualize himself in his own eyes. Through the sole fact of addressing another, the one who is speaking of himself installs the other in himself, and thereby apprehends himself, confronts himself, and establishes himself as he aspires to be, and finally historicizes himself in this incomplete or falsified history. [3]

It would be hard to find a more suggestive account of Richard's discursive motivation, and only a few supplementary comments are called for. First, "to individualize himself in his own eyes" is a minor aspect of the motivational drama, though if we replace "individualize" with "stage" and add the eyes of others, it becomes more significant. Second, the sense of the phrase "apprehends himself" may be augmented to include "fears or dreads (is apprehensive of) himself." Consequently, third, it is not always clear whether Richard is confronting himself or evading himself or, more confusedly, doing both at once. Fourth, the statement that he "establishes himself as he aspires to be" should be given a subversive interpretation inasmuch as he seems for the most part (not always) to aspire to be contemned, deposed, dead, damned, and buried in the falsified history of Richard he concocts for present and future audiences.

These introductory remarks should indicate that I don't place much stock in the often repeated opinion that Richard is a solipsist. His performance in 3.2 makes it clear that he is no mere dandy, trapped in metaphor and refining his own sensibility out of existence. From the beginning of the scene he makes himself a spectacle, as if to test the limits of the protection against scorn, the limits of the incentives to flattery and deference, that royal dignity offers. After the introductory exchange of phatic remarks identifies the occasion as Richard's debarking in Wales from Ireland, he does not continue to engage his interlocutors directly. Instead he makes them an audience, turning away to perform his apostrophe to the earth for their benefit. This device intensifies a quality his speech assumes when we read it with imaginary audition attuned to its theatrical as well as its dramatic dimensions—when, that is, we distinguish analytically between its character as performance before a theater audience and its character as utterance to fictional interlocutors. The quality is histrionic awareness: the sense conveyed by Richard's language that he is striking rhetorical postures for effect and that he is monitoring the response—scrutinizing his auditors, listening to them listen—as he speaks.

Richard's histrionic awareness was first given serious attention in 1952 by Georges Bonnard in an article that contains what I think is still the best summary description of the protagonist's performance in 3.2.[4] I quote it at some length, for that reason but also because it can serve as a run-through of the material I shall be decelerating for closer analysis. Bonnard begins the account by observing that Richard's "theatrical greeting of his kingdom on disembarking near Barkloughly Castle" and his "elaborate attitudes" are

> premeditated actions. But when Aumerle bluntly tells him he had better get down to work, how wonderfully he can play the offended sovereign rebuking his followers for doubting the power and the will of Heaven to protect "the anointed king"! That such

protestations are insubstantial, merely assumed for the moment, is vividly brought home to all by his turning pale at the news of the dispersal of Salisbury's Welshmen and confessing his help-lessness, but a word of Aumerle suffices to remind him of his part as the bearer of a name that cannot but awe and defeat his ene-mies. Thereupon Scroop approaches with more bad news, and Richard now enters as eagerly into the part of the man who is prepared for the worst, who is ready to bow to fate in perfect resignation. But this new attitude is no less insincere, no less merely acted than the previous one, as we realize almost at once when, by telling him that his favorites have made their peace with Bolingbroke, Scroop causes him to flare up into a brief orgy of invectives, and thus betray his true self, before he can understand that they have been executed. His histrionic nature, however, quickly reasserts itself. He sees, and catches at, the opportunity of acting the moralist, the philosopher, the king who refuses to be honored as a king because he knows he is no better . . . than his fellow-men. (98–99)

This attention to the histrionic profile of the scene picks out the dimension on which the following commentary will focus, al-though—since it is guided by very different interests and presup-positions—my reading will produce a portrait of Richard radi-cally different from Bonnard's. His explanation of Richard's histrionic bent is the traditional one:

> In Richard's case, absence of character combines with incompe-tence as a ruler to make a "poseur" of him. He is all sensibility and imagination, but he has no strength of mind, no common sense, no grasp of reality, . . . in short none of the qualities that constitute character. . . . His is, to some extent at least, an artist's nature. . . . Insecure, deprived of any inward guidance, he cannot possibly let others see him as he really is, and, debarred from appearing his weak, uncertain, vacillating self, what can he do but pretend to be what he is not, but live as an actor on the stage? (96)

The writer of this passage exhibits sympathy for the sources of embarrassment that make Richard an actor, but he also exhibits embarrassment himself. I mention this reflex of bourgeois dis-dain because it is symptomatic of a pattern of response the Ricar-dian performance elicits: it raises the question of how to situate oneself before the performance and interpret the response. Should we be embarrassed for Shakespeare as well as for Richard? Do we judge Shakespeare to be embarrassed by Richard—to have written his embarrassment into the part? Does he represent Richard as embarrassed by Richard? And as practicing the art of embarrassing others?

The two passages quoted above contain a contradiction that provides a clue to the problem. On the one hand, Bonnard writes that Richard can't possibly expose "his weak, uncertain, vacillating self" but must "pretend to be what he is not." On the other hand, his survey of the series of roles enacted by Richard produces the impression of an actor who stages weakness, uncertainty, and vacillation, an actor who represents himself to his auditors as "all sensibility and imagination," as lacking "strength of mind" and "common sense," and as having a spectacularly weak "grasp of reality." Richard may well *be* (represented by Shakespeare as) a "poseur," but the question implied by the contradiction is whether he *represents himself* as a "poseur" and, if so, to whom and why. In order to answer such questions we have to look more closely at the play's language, and at the same time we have to factor in—more fully than Bonnard has done—the dialogical play of speech and audition taking place between Richard and his interlocutors. The language indeed creates a speaker who enjoys discomfiting his audience with unexpected or embarrassing moves and with blather calculated to try their patience so that whatever ceremonial politeness they display must seem like flattery.

The opening lines of the apostrophe are a case in point:

> Dear earth, I do salute thee with my hand,
> Though rebels wound thee with their horses' hoofs.
> As a long-parted mother with her child
> Plays fondly with her tears and smiles in meeting,
> So weeping, smiling, greet I thee, my earth,
> And do thee favors with my royal hands . . .
>
> (3.2.6–11)

The antitheses of the salute promise an appropriately regal and restorative response: "I" against "rebels," "salute" against "wound," and "hand" against "hoofs." He comes to the motherland bearing peace and reverence, not the sword. But when the motherland becomes his child, strange things begin to happen, not least of which is a second untoward reversal. As he kneels down (one assumes) to do his manual favors he seems to regress to childhood and rematernalize the earth,[5] for he beseeches her in her traditional role of nurturant: let her not feed his foe; let the toxic powers imbibed by some of her less appealing productions be mobilized on his behalf; let her command an ambush of the horses' hooves,

> let thy spiders that suck up thy venom
> And heavy-gaited toads lie in their way,
> Doing annoyance to the treacherous feet,
> Which with usurping steps do trample thee;
> Yield stinging nettles to mine enemies . . .
> (14–18)

The signal flashed by "usurping" only intensifies the sense of impotence announced by so modest a muster of underbrush irregulars. Worried loyalists doubtless audit this mumbo-jumbo for some coded reference to a more serious form of insidious lurking power, some table of metaphoric conversion to nonmagical armament, some clue that Richard has more up his sleeve or in his crown than spiders, toads, and nettles. But the image remains grounded in detail whose accent is on the small, the squashable, the slow-moving, the passivity of "lie" (here helpless to release its pun), and the uneasy pliability of "Yield." Well before he learns of his favorites' execution or of the defection of the Welshmen and York, he is positioning himself for defeat and dramatizing the futility of a military response.[6] Like a superstitious child whose worm's-eye view magnifies diminutives, Richard implores the help of tiny guerrillas clearly inadequate to their charge. He will change his rhetorical mode when the apostrophe continues, but so far both the tonal and the figural emphasis is on feminine vulnerability, softness, and weakness.

This emphasis is rendered even more mawkish by its contrast to the martial setting that the stage directions give: *"Drums: Flourish and Colours. Enter Richard, Aumerle, Carlile and Soldiers"* (Folio). As a cue to the scene of audition, this prepares us to imagine the way Richard's speech "listens" to the effects it produces. There are, of course, other ways to interpret the cue. Potter, for example, argues that Richard's characteristic irony is absent from this scene and that the presence of Carlisle helps account for the difference: Richard becomes "spokesman for England and the Church. From the moment when he greets the English earth, it is he alone who embodies the spirit of Mowbray's lament for his native tongue, Bolingbroke's 'English ground, farewell', and Gaunt's famous purple passage." His behavior in the scene is not "an undignified oscillation between two equally reprehensible states of mind, futile rage and morbid despair." Rather, it is "a bringing out into the open of a conflict between two equally valid but contradictory roles of king and Christian" ("Antic Disposition," 36). This, however, is to screen out his antic play with the equally valid but contradictory roles of child and mother, or those of woman and man. And it is also to screen out the imagined auditory context that helps us establish the mood of the speaker's histrionic awareness. If we listen with Carlisle's ears we can hardly resist the suspicion that Richard is out to secure the soldierly bishop's disapproval. No doubt he teases Carlisle with a version of the Christian motif of power in meekness. But it is a studiedly feminized, infantile, and pagan travesty of the motif. He flaunts his unwillingness to resist physical force, and we shall see that Carlisle's response ratifies the efficacy of this posture.

When the apostrophe continues, however, the posture is modified, or at least complicated, by an adjustment of figural weight from magical incantation toward allegorical metaphor:

> And when they from thy bosom pluck a flower,
> Guard it, I pray thee, with a lurking adder,
> Whose double tongue may with a mortal touch
> Throw death upon thy sovereign's enemies.
> (3.2.19–22)

The shift of focus to a single moment and action ("when they pluck") combines with the indefinite singular ("*a* flower," "*a* lurking adder") to distinguish this scene from the plural and participially diffuse activity of spiders, toads, feet, and nettles. The parabolic edge is sharper, more arch: which flower? which adder? Even more dramatically than a host of flowers, a single flower displays its defenselessness along with its fragile, short-lived beauty and asks to be plucked; and since it promises easy picking its fanciers can dispense with the violence of trampling cavalries. The image offers up Richard and the crown as its easiest referent, compressing in a seductive figure the feminine nuances of his self-representation.

These lines are duplicitous, and so Richard resembles the adder as well. The appearance, in the third line, of the play's most pervasive weapon indicates a correlation between his floral vulnerability and the power of his double tongue. Richard is not asking earth to prevent the flower from being plucked, since the adder is to lurk, and since "guard" means "trim" or "line" as well as "watch over."[7] He expects the flower to be plucked, and the temporal construction proposes that event as the prerequisite to the adder's bite. His revenge, his spiritual triumph over his enemies, is contingent on his political defeat; so also is the working out of the revenge he takes upon himself. His forked tongue will flick outward to touch Bolingbroke with its venom ("Here, cousin, seize the crown"), but it also doubles back upon the nearest of his enemies, himself. Lines 19–22 thus contain Richard's scenario in a nutshell. But for whose benefit is this parable of the flower and the adder uttered? Its forked meaning does not appear to be caught by his auditors or to have been intended for their ears. I shall return to this question after glancing at the conclusion of the speech.

Richard appears to dismiss the whole apostrophe when his "tune goes manly" in the final four lines,[8] and he pledges steadfast resistance:

> Mock not my senseless conjuration, lords:
> This earth shall have a feeling, and these stones
> Prove armed soldiers ere her native king
> Shall falter under foul rebellion's arms.
>
> (23–26)

"Senseless" has been taken to modify both the conjurer and the conjuree.[9] The latter is the obvious first choice, but since the negative injunction suggests Richard's awareness that mockery might be appropriate, the former is also plausible: the term may denote the neglectful, irrational, or foolish quality of his conjuring. All he really meant to suggest, he now claims, was that he would, if necessary, resort to royal magic, would recruit and sensitize the natural world to his cause, before deigning to submit to rebellion; the apostrophe was only a melodramatic way to express his will to persevere. This revised interpretation of his performance is of course blatantly senseless and mischievous, not least in leaving open the possibility that if push came to shove earth's native king and mother might subject her, the stones, and his audience to another such conjuration. If someone concerned for the welfare of king and country detects a note of mockery, perhaps of self-mockery, in the speech, he may well be skeptical of the king's promise not to falter.

But who is this someone? For whose benefit, to repeat my question, does Richard perform? What motivates so unsettling a self-representation? The questions take us back to the issue of the reader's imaginary audition and to the problem of defining its dimensions more precisely than I did earlier when I mentioned the distinction between theatrical performance and fictional utterance. To illustrate the problem, I cite G. R. Hibbard's response to "Mock not my senseless conjuration, lords": this is "both a concealed stage direction, demanding that those about Richard make some sort of gesture expressing impatience, and also a sign to the audience to take note of his tendency towards verbal self-indulgence and excess." [10] The second clause both raises and begs the important question. *Which* audience? And *whose* sign? The answer demanded by Hibbard's commitment to the narrative that organizes his study, the fiction of development, is that the sign is Shakespeare's and the audience the theater audience. This narrative prevents him from entertaining seriously what his words suggest: that Richard is staging himself and at the same time prompting his onstage audience to mock his performance. Hibbard insists that "the poetry Richard speaks is Shakespeare's, not his" (115), and delivers the same opinion about his theatricality. Shakespeare, he argues, brilliantly justifies his penchant for writing "self-consciously beautiful speeches" by adapting this facility "to a theatrical purpose." Speeches composed "with more than a touch of self-indulgence" somehow manage to bring out "one of Richard's worst failings as a man and still more as a king: his readiness to find a refuge in words, which grow ever more remote from the business in hand. . . . Shakespeare has it both ways: he writes the poetry he wants to write, and he makes his own critical attitude to that poetry serve also as a criticism of his hero" (119). In its general form Hibbard's developmental approach is the same as John Baxter's in *Shakespeare's Poetic Styles,* and it is symptomatic of the methodological flaw built into the approach that although their assessments of Shakespeare's success in having it both ways are very much at odds with each other, they derive those assessments from a common tendency to explain the character's moral problems in terms of the playwright's esthetic struggle with his material, a tendency that entails a persistent confusion between fictional and theatrical effects.[11]

We could well expect more light on the problem to be cast by those who employ a metatheatrical rather than a developmental paradigm. Unconstrained by the need to equate later works with greater works, they are also in a better position to explore and appreciate the ways the effects of theater can operate interpretively within the boundaries of dramatic fiction. *Richard II* has always been a metatheatrical favorite because it lends itself so readily to studies of the Player King, but during the past few decades a strong tradition has developed that I think has unduly limited the interpretive force and variety inherent in the paradigm. Its main thesis: Richard's awareness that he is only acting increases during the play until he is paralyzed by the sense that he is living a dream or an illusion; as an actor is separated from his part, and a name from its referent, so Richard becomes separated from his royal role and his self, conceiving both as mere fictions.[12] But if he is an actor, he must be in search of an audience, and most of the innumerable metatheatrical studies of Richard do not throw much light on the particular object of that search. They add little to the insights contained in Barton's *Shakespeare and the Idea of the Play.* Barton classifies Richard as one of "the

Player Kings of the flawed rule"—imperfect kings in whom the contrast is so marked between the individual and the role of king "that it evokes the image of the actor" (121). From the third act on Richard gets increasingly pathetic, losing his initially firm "confidence in the inviolability of kingship" along with his "hold upon the crown," and as he comes to view his reign as an illusion "the image of the actor pursues" him "relentlessly"—until the death scene, when he makes a last-minute comeback (123–26). Barton's thematic focus on theatricality was pathbreaking but it was also costly: exhibits of the leading idea are too often produced by transplanting passages from their native interlocutory habitat to the thin soil of the thematic display case.

This procedure plagues much "meta-"criticism—metatheatrical, metadramatic, metapoetic—and prompts its practitioners to take Richard's self-descriptions at face value because it abstracts from both the motivational drama inscribed in the text and the auditory drama embedded in finite stretches of dialogue. Richard becomes merely pathetic. Thus Calderwood maintains that he "lapses into . . . lyric narcissism" in 3.2: his "sentimental verbal kingdoms are gratifying to him because within their imagined borders he holds uncontested sway" (*Metadrama,* 25). But a phrase such as "mock not" is contextualized in a manner that throws this reading in question. Its negative form is self-canceling because it draws attention to something the speaker proclaims mockworthy. Since he consistently indexes his "verbal kingdoms" in this fashion, he doesn't simply "lapse" into narcissism. He displays it. And he displays it *as* a "lapse," anticipating and even soliciting Calderwood's disapproval: "See how gratifying my sentimental verbal kingdoms are to me!" The fact that this disapproval is shared by Richard's onstage auditors is a symptom of the problem: the critic responds *as if* Richard speaks directly to him and to the extrafictional audience or readership at large, but since he knows this is not the case—knows he is not present to Richard—he has no reason to assume Richard is staging himself, much less staging himself as a target. The critic therefore concludes that his real transaction is not with the character but with the author: "Richard's sentimental, magical investment in royal semantics metaphorically reflects Shakespeare's own artistic investment in the poetic mode. . . . Not that Richard in any blunt sense 'is' Shakespeare . . . for it is Shakespeare, after all, who supplies us with a critique of Richard's position" (5), an assertion that puts Calderwood in the same camp as Hibbard, and for the same reasons. When the critic bypasses and replaces the onstage auditors he has no means of entry into the interlocutory drama, and this in turn blocks his access to the textual representation of the motivational drama, which in Richard's case centers on the drama of self-auscultation.

Some of the problems confronting this approach have been handled more successfully in Blanpied's recent study of the history plays. Blanpied takes a step forward by trying to link the "meta-"themes more closely to the specific topic of Richard's drive to self-destruction and by examining the effect of this linkage on Richard's sense of audience.[13] His is in many ways a superior and exemplary version of recent metatheatrical criticism. It is superior because he directly addresses the question of Richard's histrionic awareness in a reading that produces valuable insights. It is exemplary because his response to the question still exhibits the weaknesses that lie in the theoretical foundations of the approach, but it does so in a form that will reward scrutiny and revision. In the pages that follow I shall try to clarify the outlines of my own metatheatrical commitments through a critique of Blanpied's approach.

Blanpied acknowledges and displays his debt to the work of Burckhardt and Calderwood. Like them, he tends to assimilate the actor/character analogy to the character/playwright analogy. For example, he explores the way the figure of the king expresses the double concern of the dramatist with "the integrity and coherence of the historical world" in the fiction and with its theatrical credibility, its orientation "toward the audience, to whom he [the king] 'carries across' the living drama" (13). The king, Blanpied argues, is both a manipulative machiavel who weaves plots and a self-delighting antic performer who engages the audience and reveals "all the machiavel's works as theatrical illusion" (14); a "strange and exhilarating" figure bridging the void between the two worlds of fiction and theater. This places him in a treacherous position: "To be at home in the theater is to be a stranger in the fiction, a faker of the role of king, and to be found out. We perceive him coming toward us, stepping forward from among his fellows and inevitably drawing their attention to his falseness" (120).

The interpretive practice based on this hypothesis produces a strong reading of histrionic awareness, and one that provides an instructive contrast against which to define my own model. The problems I want to raise can be focused by putting three questions to the quoted passage that concludes the preceding paragraph: Whose perception does the first sentence ("To be at home . . .") express? By whom is the king "found out"? Why and how does his "coming toward us" draw *his fellows'* attention to his falseness? The general question behind these questions of course concerns the epistemic relation Blanpied posits between the theater audience and the character's awareness. Are we really present to the character, does he perform for our benefit, monitor our responses, watch and listen to the way we watch and listen? Blanpied's account of the apostrophe shows how he resolves these questions: Richard returns from Ireland "with a new language of his own, in a nerve-quickened state of freedom and horror" occasioned by "a sense of dispossession." Whether or not he knows on his reentry "how powerless he is, he talks as if he did," as if "he detected *our* knowledge of his powerlessness. In his new stage-presence his ears are unstopped, he seems to be listening for sounds *beyond* his fictive enclosure, responding to *our* sense of his absurdity" (125, my italics). He plays, but he plays "feelingly," striking "outrageous postures" that are not so much expressions of hypocrisy as "experiments" and "improvisations," and this

is a very perilous strategy. The manic behavior—the absurd bravado, sudden despair, the affectation, wily pathos, rhetorical craziness—attests to Richard's nakedness, but it also strains *our* patience. . . . So he pitches himself *to us blindly, across a very real void, sensing our presence but not, after all, knowing it or able to identify it.* Nor has he the luxury of the fiction of direct address, the too easy gesture of confidence. To "soliloquize" *us* directly would be to beg for *our* special protection, to neutralize the risk he takes. (126)

The italics, all of which are mine, pick out the phrases that seem to me to confuse what are otherwise genuine insights into Richard's performance. Blanpied carries Richard and his awareness across the void so precipitously that he bypasses the onstage cues to its motivating conditions—bypasses, for example, such sounds and presences *within* the fictive enclosure as trumpets, drums, colors, soldiers, and the Bishop of Carlisle.

The Bishop responds to Richard with a mild but tight-lipped reproof that rescues the manly tune from the King's pagan mothering and restores its Christian paternity. Carlisle shows himself not fully persuaded by Richard's final promise. His words register the effect of the "senseless conjuration" by the terse and measured sternness with which they fend off that self-indulgent effusion:

> Fear not, my lord. That power that made you king
> Hath power to keep you king in spite of all.
> The means that heaven yields must be imbrac'd
> And not neglected; else, heaven would,
> And we will not; heavens offer, we refuse
> The proffered means of succour and redress.
> $(3.2.27-32)$

Whether or not Richard strains *our* patience or appeals and responds to *our* sense of his absurdity seems less important at this point than two other considerations: his effect on the *Bishop*'s patience and sense of his absurdity, and the effect of the Bishop's words on Richard's subsequent behavior. Carlisle offers instruction, and Aumerle clarifies it, as if lecturing a child: the former speaks primarily to the lavish display of softness and weakness at the beginning of the apostrophe.[14] His exhortation is therefore moral rather than practical, and his reference to "proffered means" offered by heaven is vague enough to prompt Aumerle to spell the admonition out in more realistic terms:

> He means, my lord, that we are too remiss;
> Whilst Bolingbroke, through our security,
> Grows strong and great in substance and in power.
> $(33-35)$

This exchange tempts me to entertain a brief image of Richard eyeing the Bishop with a certain wry wonder at the confidence the latter displays in heaven and with a certain amused curiosity about the Bishop's ideas as to how Richard is to embrace and implement the heavenly offer of help. He may also be imagined to have his own private view of the problem of "security"— neglect of means—for the "searching eye of heaven" speech that follows responds with bombastic disregard of practical danger and delineates his reaction to the Bishop's advice.[15] The speech both dodges the practical issue, and mocks Carlisle's restrictively military use of religious ideology, by shifting it to the moral register:

> Discomfortable cousin! know'st thou not
> That when the searching eye of heaven is hid
> Behind the globe and lights the lower world,
> Then thieves and robbers range abroad unseen
> In murthers and in outrage boldly here;
> But when from under this terrestrial ball
> He fires the proud tops of the eastern pines,
> And darts his light through every guilty hole,
> Then murthers, treasons, and detested sins,
> The cloak of night being pluck'd from off their backs,
> Stand bare and naked, trembling at themselves?
> So when this thief, this traitor, Bolingbroke,
> Who all this while hath revell'd in the night,
> Whilst we were wand'ring with the Antipodes,
> Shall see us rising in our throne the east,
> His treasons will sit blushing in his face,
> Not able to endure the sight of day,
> But self-affrighted tremble at his sin.
>
> (36–53)

This speech is asking for trouble, and the critics are quick to respond: "His argument could hardly be more magnificent—or more irrelevant"; "a sort of *wordy* courage that betrays the inward impotence"; "his tendency towards fantasies of omnipotence. . . . Now that he has returned from the Antipodes, treason and conspiracy will be dissolved by his mere appearance"; threatened with insurrection he "chooses to do little more than chastise Aumerle for lack of faith in the efficacy of the sunking concept."[16]

These criticisms seem at first glance to be justified by the self-indulgent violence of the rhetoric assimilating Richard to divine and solar power, figuring him as a scourge, a basilisk eye, a harrower, an agent of judgment and retribution who burns down the trees to flush out guilty souls hiding like animals. But "trembling at themselves" strikes a different chord—one might have expected "trembling at the sun"—as does "self-affrighted tremble at his sin." Here the emphasis is on self-judgment and self-affright rather than public exposure and fear of punishment. "Know'st thou not?"—"isn't it obvious?", obvious to anyone who peers out at life from within the guilty worm-eaten hole of conscience; who knows what Richard knows. S. K. Heninger notes that Richard's reference to the sun-king concept "recalls a standard of kingly conduct which points up the immoralities that Acts I and II so fulsomely reveal"; hence when he applies the image to himself it "becomes an ironical epithet that emphasizes his failure as God's deputy" (324). Yet if this is so, it may reflect as much on "the efficacy of the sun-king concept" as on the incumbent; he may be chastising Aumerle (*and* Carlisle) not for lack of faith but, rather, for faith in its efficacy. Acts 1 and 2 don't merely reveal his "immoralities," they reveal him flaunting them, even relishing them. Thus if the epithet is "ironical" the irony must be Richard's as well as Shakespeare's. Perhaps his own "murthers, treasons, and detested sins"—the murder of Gloucester, the theft of the Lancastrian inheritance, the depredations mentioned by Gaunt and others—tremble self-affrighted before his searching eye. And perhaps he savors his self-affright, hoarding it, hiding it from others.

Crossing athwart Richard's language is an echo of Faust's rhetoric of despair in the last scene of *Doctor Faustus*. The echo increases the inflationary billow and lines his language with complex self-mockery: mockery not only at the speaker for assuming his solar divinity but also at the formulas of divinely sanctioned kingship and at those who think to protect, console, or deceive themselves with them. The edge is sharpened by the interchangeability of the predicaments that characterize the two principals: the exiled Bolingbroke returned from his "wand'ring"; the wastrel king to whom the normal sense of "revell'd in the night" applies more aptly than to Bolingbroke. At this moment Richard's threat may indeed seem to be idle, "irrelevant," and wish-fulfilling, a testimony to his political "impotence." But if, as critics are fond of insisting, Richard is a *Player* King, why shouldn't we imagine that "political impotence" is an effect he *stages,* rehearsing it in this scene and performing it in the next in so forceful a manner as to deny the vacillating Bolingbroke a fallback position and compel him to take it all?—to Bolingbroke's "My gracious lord, I come but for mine own," Richard replies, "Your own is yours, and I am yours, and all" (3.3.196–97). The "all" Richard transmits to Bolingbroke includes within the hollow crown not only his own death but also the resurrection and gradual increase of his corrosive moral influence boring at Henry from within. Richard's guilty self-understanding first infects Henry in the buried fear presented by Exton, flares up in the king's encounters with his son, and waxes through two plays in a long slow moral dying.

The blustery display of the "Discomfortable cousin" speech is doubly self-fulfilling: it helps bring on the political impotence it stages, and it proleptically encodes an emblem of Richard's permanent effect on his heir and usurper. Thus whetted, its mockery bites deep into the pious reassurances Richard goes on to intone:

> Not all the water in the rough rude sea
> Can wash the balm off from an anointed king;
> The breath of worldly men cannot depose
> The deputy elected by the Lord . . .
>
> (54–57)

Andrew Gurr reads this as political foolhardiness: "a blunt refusal to acknowledge Bullingbrook's flood." [17] But it is tonally, logically, and motivationally more complex than that. On the one hand, the first two lines imply that there will be no "balm" for "rough rude" Bolingbroke even if he prevails, while the second two lines leave open the possibility that although only the Lord has the authority to depose an anointed king, he may delegate that to the deputy who represents his spiritual commands to worldly subjects. But, on the other hand, the echo of Bolingbroke's "to wash your blood / From off my hands," uttered in the previous scene (3.1.5–6), confirms the rhetorical misfire of the first two lines, stuffing "guilt" or "blood" under the cloak of "balm." The echo can't be intentional, since Richard was absent from that scene, but its message to us is clear: Richard does not fully succeed in displacing his accusatory rhetoric from himself to Bolingbroke, and we may deduce from his tonal mockery that he may not want to.

That rhetoric continually tongues the canker that produced it, searches out the trembling self-affrighted sinner within, and solicits the punishment that will serve him right. His conclusion is nothing if not a mordant parody that mimics Bishop-talk, reducing Carlisle's plea for action to an argument for remaining inactive and leaving it to heaven:

> The breath of worldly men cannot depose
> The deputy elected by the Lord;
> For every man that Bolingbroke hath press'd
> To lift shrewd steel against our golden crown,
> God for his Richard hath in heavenly pay
> A glorious angel: then, if angels fight,
> Weak men must fall, for heaven still guards the right.
> (56–62)

In short, if "heaven would," let it. So much for Aumerle's "security" and the spiritual athleticism of the *miles ecclesiae*. Carlisle's catechizing from the Credo of heavenly means is here sent up by inflation and sent back down in a shower of gold. The image of apocalyptic hope suffers from the low rate of the witty exchange that converts it to a coin-tossing contest and perhaps glances at one of the earthly means always in short supply. The transactions between king and clergy that open *Henry V* suggest the particular kind of succor and redress Richard finds missing in the Bishop's offer.[18]

What marks this as bitter mockery is not merely the hysterical witplay but also the emphasis, in the preceding lines of the speech, on self-judgment and self-affright that I discussed above. Directed inward as well as outward, the mockery is consistent with that displayed in the "senseless conjuration" of the apostrophe. Richard has merely borrowed a page from the Bishop's book and shifted his conjuration from earth to heaven and from the maternal to the paternal register. But he does so in tones that test the limits of impiety, in language that generates a much more complex and nuanced self-representation than his auditors appear to grasp. Perhaps his foursquare Christianity shelters the Bishop from hearing those tones. If the fact that neither he nor anyone else expressly comments on Richard's perverse mimicry is taken as an indication of selective or imperfect audition, this only makes it more perverse. For one is then forced to conclude that Richard revels in creating what Bertrand Evans calls "discrepant awarenesses,"[19] engaging in a kind of aggressive auditory voyeurism that is another manifestation of the adder's double tongue.

The idea that Richard is an auditory voyeur takes us back to Blanpied's study, because it suggests that his metatheatrical explanation of histrionic awareness is, on the face of it, plausible. He responds to the felt necessity of positing another audience to whom Richard communicates those meanings that escape his onstage interlocutors. Since, for example, the apostrophe to earth is (literally) a turning away from fictive auditors, he assumes that it must be directed across the edge of the stage to the theatrical audience. But in doing so, as I noted, he bypasses the onstage cues provided by the interplay of successive utterances that contextualize any particular speech act. The consequence of this move is that he deprives himself of the material for a coherent dramatic explanation of Richard's behavior and replaces it with a metatheatrical account that is less an interpretation of the play than a rationalization for its dramatic defects. I want to explore this strategy in order to underline the theoretical differences between the metatheatrical approach pursued by Burckhardt, Calderwood, and Blanpied, and the approach I am proposing here.

If Blanpied's passage from fiction to theater and from onstage to offstage audience is premature, it is because he allows his interest in the actor/character analogy to be contaminated by an interest in the character/playwright analogy.[20] This contamination shifts the interpretive focus from the theatricality of relationships "within" dramatic fiction to the actual structure of the theatrical relationships "around" dramatic fiction.[21] The Player King becomes the model of the dramatist and his relations to play, players, characters, audience, and his own career. Fiction is construed as the vehicle and theater the tenor.

A certain evaluative commitment is implicated in this construal. Blanpied punctuates a series of trenchant observations on Richard's problematic display of self-pity and its relation to his power with another series of remarks that develop the same double hypothesis as the one adopted by G. R. Hibbard (see pp. 83–84, above): that the play is flawed, and that Shakespeare discerned the flaws and inscribed his critique in the language and dramaturgy of the fifth act.

> Having reached a cul-de-sac with Richard himself, he now seeks to dramatize the problems that thwart the tragic self-declaring impulse of the play. The overt ambiguities of the ending project the play's fundamental irresolution, which makes it finally impossible to say whether Richard reveals an inner emptiness or the play itself can simply go no further in its self-consuming momentum. This blurring of the source of experience makes for a richly indeterminate play. . . . Nevertheless, the indeterminacy rests upon a mechanism of deception [i.e., that some true grief is hidden behind Richard's "external manners of lament"]. The ending is characteristically Shakespearean in its recourse to parody as a way of exposing the mechanism and, in effect, destroying its efficacy.[22]

Blanpied argues that although Richard "performs for us" and "appeals to us (of course indirectly) to sanction his show of grief" in the last three acts, although he tries to compel us "by the drama of his self-sacrifice" (129), although he projects his suffering "inwardness" toward us, we remain uncertain about the authenticity of his pain.[23] Since he controls his world and grief with a rhetorical "vigor [that] belies his claim of nothingness," he fails to persuade us that "he has earned his privileged mode of utterance," and we are forced to conclude that it derives not from "some original reality of his own" but from "Shakespeare, king of shadows, furtively inspiring his favorite" (131, 133). In Richard's Pomfret soliloquy, the dramatist parodies "his own capacity for self-deceit and self-indulgent lyricism, . . . his own underlying affinity with Richard," and "his own attempt to control the field of the play's sensations—and through them, our reactions—by defusing that control through Richard's personal style" (139). Blanpied thus claims to be collaborating with Shakespeare in converting the drama of Richard's flawed rule over England to the drama of Shakespeare's flawed rule over *Richard II*. Shakespeare displays his recognition that Richard has been straining *our* patience from the beginning and making *us* accomplices in his self-destruction: he is "the one we want and need to kill"; Exton then becomes both the "materialization of our wishes" (261) and Shakespeare's revenge on his own "gratifying identification with his protagonist" (140).

The first premise of this argument is that the play as dramatic fiction needed to be saved, and the second is that Shakespeare, seeing what Blanpied sees, managed a last-minute comeback by a critique in which he exposes the dramaturgy responsible for Richard's uneasy negotiation with a dissatisfied theater audience. Now it is clear that the second premise presupposes the first, for if the play doesn't need to be saved the metatheatrical hypothesis that relocates the scene of drama in the authorial protagonist's struggle with his character, play, and audience would seem to be gratuitous. The first premise in turn presupposes a set of interpretive decisions whose common orientation is, as I have tried to show, a tendency to bypass onstage cues and relationships. In Richard's apostrophe, in the speeches that succeed it, and—as we shall see—in all the play's textual and dialogical transactions, there is evidence for a positive reading of precisely those ambiguities, indeterminacies, mechanisms of deceptions, and so forth that Blanpied treats as defects. What he considers to be flaws in the theatrical register of character/audience relations, I find to be compelling effects in the fictional register of character/character relations. If I am correct in claiming that such evidence exists, then Blanpied's argument is circular, since he faults the play for lacking the justifying evidence his metatheatrical commitment leads him to ignore.

It is nevertheless the case that Blanpied's insights severally yield up a powerful interpretation of Richard when shifted to the fictional register, and I find myself in the uncomfortable position of doing to his reading what he tries to do to Shakespeare's play. I think everything he says about Richard's performance per se is valuable and important in its descriptive (as distinct from its evaluative) dimension. I thoroughly endorse the view that Richard imposes his "outrageous postures," his "inwardness," and his "drama of . . . self-sacrifice" on his audience in ways that are embarrassing and question "the authenticity" of his pain; the view that he is the source of much that can be considered bad theater; and the view that his histrionic awareness of the effects his performance produces is highly developed. For Blanpied, the question is, "How far are we willing to be implicated, how far persuaded, how far willing to fortify him with our sympathy and belief?" (129), and the answer to the question—"very willing" or "unwilling"—determines his judgment of the play's relative success. The question in itself is legitimate, since what we are reading or observing is a play. But in my opinion it is mis- directed, and the negative answer it solicits points not to a defec- tive quality in the play but to a coherently motivated effect which the play represents Richard as seeking to produce. Not, however, on "us," and here I would like to underscore the casual paren- thesis in Blanpied's statement that Richard "appeals to us (of course indirectly) to sanction his show of grief." How indirectly? Entirely indirectly, which is to say that from a certain standpoint he doesn't appeal to "us" at all, since he can't know "we" exist. From this standpoint, the question should be rephrased by replac- ing "we," "him," and "our" with shifters that denote Richard and his interlocutors. Yet this is not an entirely satisfactory solution. Although the rephrasing may produce salutary interpretive re- sults, the total exclusion of the audience is wrongheaded, be- cause the question "How far are *we* willing to be implicated?" has an essential symptomatic function, and the problem is how to conceptualize it so as to avoid the kind of interpretive bypass encouraged by the metatheatrical emphasis on playwright and audience. The following reflections address themselves to the problem.

In his recent study of the phenomenology of theater, Bert States remarks that Shakespearean drama easily accommodates the mimetic or representational principle to what he calls the collaborative principle: "the illusionary realness of Shakespeare's theater . . . always contains a subtle collaborative element, or at least an option to address the audience," and States speculates that "the function of this option was not simply to allow the play to acknowledge its own fictionality, but to keep one theatrical eye on the very palpable crowd ringing the stage."[24] In the collaborative mode, "theater says to the spectator, 'Why should we pretend that all this is an illusion. We are in this together'" (181). But when this occurs in conjunction with the representational mode, the "we" is restricted, for if "the actor plays a character who lives in a world that includes the audience,"

> the actor who plays to the audience in the aside or the monologue is usually well within the play world, since the audience he addresses is only the idea of an audience. The audience actually has the status of a confidant character in neoclassical tragedy, unlike the real audience that modern participation theater tries to involve quite literally in the play.   (170–71)

> When Edmund collaboratively lets us in on his play [*sic*] to undo his brother, we are still well within the illusionary world of *King Lear* which includes (for certain characters at least) access to an imaginary listener. We are, in fact, only one short step beyond soliloquy, in which the character tends to speak as much about himself as to himself.   (184)

What States is saying is both clear and reasonable, yet the slipperiness inherent in the concepts that underlie his modal distinctions destabilize some of his assertions in interesting ways.

I note first the volatility of the statement, "Why should we pretend that all this is an illusion," which can mean the same as its negation and continually reverses itself, like the Necker cube, partly because the coupling of "illusion" with "pretend" intensifies the ambiguity of the former ("Why should we make believe that all this is make-believe?") and partly because shifting the accent of the rhetorical question from "illusion" to "pretend" ("Why shouldn't we *believe* . . .") opens up another set of problems.

Second, is it the actor or the character "who plays *to* the audience"? If it is the actor as character, and if the character plays to the audience qua audience, then doesn't the character assume the role of "actor" and the audience of "audience" in the character's "world"? In what sense is this "the idea of an audience" rather than a fictive audience consisting of spectators playing the role of "spectator" in the character's "world"? And doesn't participation theater convert its real audience to a "real audience" in similar fashion? If one function of the collaborative mode is "to allow the play to acknowledge its own fictionality," surely another is to comment on the playlike fictionality of such institutional roles as "real audience" and in general to comment on prevailing fictions of reality, to show that nature mirrors art and that extratheatrical institutions are penetrated, riddled, by the powers or dangers of theater.

Third, is the statement that certain characters have "access to an imaginary listener" to be construed ontologically or psychologically? Does it mean that the listener is imaginary in the same way that the character is imaginary or that the listener is imagined by the character? Who and where could that listener be? Is there any difference at all between Edmund's sharing of confidence and the act of soliloquy? Doesn't the soliloquist speak about himself to himself in the presence of someone who "has the status of a confidant character"?

What motivates these questions is an old-fashioned scruple about the need to protect the boundary between actor and character, theater and fiction, against the easy encroachment of various kinds of *meta*theories. Since I agree with States not only that Shakespeare's theater always contains "an option to address the audience" but also that it often encourages and represents that "collaborative element," I think it is vital for interpretive practice to approach the option with clear, if initially oversimple, distinctions. Where the collaborative element is a convention, the presence of the audience to the play is always latent as an effect that interpretation must take into account. The interpreter's task is to tease out the textual manifestations of the effect and to focus his response to them on the particular dramatic contingencies of the individual play. But the problem is that since the effect of audience presence (and thus of the play as play) is primarily a theatrical rather than a dramatic ingredient, its consideration tends to nudge the interpreter away from those contingencies. It encourages an interest in the interplay "between actor and audience" that gives "the spectator something more than a passive role in the theater exchange" (States, *Great Reckonings,* 170), and this—as Blanpied's practice illustrates—can easily bleed into a concern for the interplay between *character* and audience. But the perception that the audience is present to the play is only a general actuating signal the message of which is that histrionic awareness in the dramatic (fictional) community should be factored into interpretive response. If it puts us on notice that characters may have a special level of audience awareness, we needn't deduce from this that they are aware of the audience present to the actors. My objection to this move is primarily pragmatic—I think it blurs the interpreter's focus—but it also springs from a dramaturgical principle, which is that at least in the representational/collaborative mode described by States, a character in a play being performed in a theater cannot know he is a character in *that* play being performed in *that* theater. If he displays such awareness, *that* play and theater become *another* play and theater extended from, but also extending and contained within, the fictive enclosure that is all the character qua character can be aware of. The reasoning behind this assertion may be suggested by the following thought-experiment.

I imagine that as I am watching a play, at a certain moment an actor/character looks directly at me. How shall I respond? Several options are open, and the choice among them will be conditioned partly by the metatheatrical signs the play as a whole emits. If I suppose that it is the actor rather than the character who looks at me, I can either ignore his look or else assume he is picking me out as a momentary target in the audience; I might feel called upon to return the favor by acting alert, responsive, displeased, or bored, and in doing this I am free to choose a simulation that matches my actual feeling or one that hides it. Whatever I decide to do, I am playing the theatrical role of a spectator who perceives himself to be present to the actor in the physical space of the theater we share and fill. But the situation changes if I imagine that it is the character rather than the actor who looks directly at me. Then, unless I discern clear cues that the illusion is being broken and an absurdist response is appropriate, two possibilities are open to me.[25] The first is to imagine myself present to him. But if I do, it can't be in my role as representative spectator, for the fictional "world" pops up and materializes wherever his gaze lights. So I imagine myself present not as myself but as another, and not in my "world" (the theater) but in his (the fiction). If I consider this theatrically, I fancy myself playing the role of supernumerary in the cast rather than that of spectator: hearing him discourse on war or state I return his gaze as a soldier, a minor cleric, an attendant lord, perhaps. If within the fiction the character at some point presents himself as an actor reciting lines from an old play, or speaks to me of theater, or directs other characters who act roles in an amateur theatrical aimed at me and my neighbors in the pit, my specific role as supernumerary becomes that of "spectator," which is not at all identical with the role of spectator constituted by my response to the *actor's* gaze.

This is the first possibility, and it is the more flamboyant but, for my purposes, the less interesting of the two. The other is to ignore the character's gaze in the sense that I imagine myself absent; like a basilisk eye or a ray gun, his gaze bores through me and makes me vanish for its duration unless I resist it by transforming him back to the actor. To hypothesize my absence allows me to appreciate more clearly what is involved when a character displays histrionic awareness, when, in Blanpied's words, he "seems to be listening for sounds beyond his fictive enclosure, responding to our sense" of his self-display, and when he "performs for us" and "bids for our trust and our credulity" (*Time and the Artist,* 125, 129). For if "we" aren't there, someone must be; if "we" steadfastly maintain our absence while the character just as steadfastly continues to perform for someone's benefit, there is an invisible audience *for* him and we become its metaphoric vehicle.

I noted earlier the tendency of one kind of metatheatrical criticism to construe fiction as the vehicle and theater as the tenor, and I now propose a model that reverses this relationship, a strategy of reading that enables us to appropriate performance before the theater audience as the model or metaphor of the fictional speaker's performance before—whom? Before his onstage interlocutors to some extent, but above all, *before himself*.[26] When the reader first imagines the theater audience as the character's sounding board and then dissolves it into metaphor, he constitutes the character as his own addressee. This dissolution suggests a somewhat different meaning than States gives for his assertion that the audience an actor addresses in the aside or monologue "is only the idea of an audience": when the theater audience which the collaborative mode makes present to the play absents itself, that is, when reader or auditor imagines it absent, it is reduced to a sign whose referent is elsewhere. By being addressed the audience takes on interpretive significance, but at the same time the materiality of bodies in theatrical space becomes an obstacle to its signifying function. The actual audience offers a position, a directionality, that enables the character to display self-address in theatrical terms; however, it is not the character's self-address but only the actor's appeal to *his* audience, unless the signifying audience gives way to the "idea" it signifies.

The effect of this process, which may be called the textualization of the audience, is to establish the representation of a speaker who carries and addresses an audience in his mind even when alone. Soliloquy is the limiting case, and a moment's reflection will show the difference produced by textualizing its audience. Shakespearean soliloquies can be delivered (or their delivery imagined) upstage, as if they were private meditations, or downstage, as if taking the theater audience into confidence. The proper way to interpret the latter, as I see it, is to assume not that the speaker crosses the boundary from character to actor and from fictive to theatrical space but that he speaks to himself *as if* before an audience; he speaks for his own ears, audits and monitors his own speech, pronominally divides in two so as to become the receiver of his own messages. The first person may, for example, bid for the trust and credulity of the second person, or appeal to the second person to "sanction [or discredit] his show of grief" or try to persuade (or disgust) him "by the drama of his self-sacrifice." He may declaim or work through a particular argument in order to persuade himself to adopt a particular attitude. When the theater audience he addresses is textualized, the effect is to represent him as aware of *an audience within* that needs to be won over—an audience that may be skeptical, that may suspect him of rationalizing in bad faith, that may refuse to applaud or ratify his performance. The illocutionary action of soliloquy is self-directed.[27]

Just as there is an element of dialogue in soliloquy, so there may be an element of soliloquy in dialogical speech events. Many Shakespearean speakers appear to be working on themselves in this fashion while engaging in dialogue and working on interlocutors. Perhaps the most notorious and weird example is Edgar in *King Lear:* behind the protective screen of the Poor Tom discourse he beams at others, he continually explores his own motives and plays on his own feelings. Placing Richard's language in this framework of dual audition energizes Blanpied's idea that he solicits an audience "beyond his fictive enclosure." The idea becomes a basic clue to the power and strangeness of Shakespeare's portrayal because it suggests a way to approach what I referred to above as the auditory voyeurism of the adder's double tongue: Richard plays Richard before his onstage audience and he simultaneously plays Richard-playing-Richard before the interior audience; he cultivates "discrepant awareness" between the two audiences by aggressively bombarding interlocutors with more meanings than their ears are attuned to receive, and the relish he takes in his command of verse conveys the delight with which he hoards and savors the surplus.

By correlating the textualized model of the scene of theater with the close textual analysis of language, I arrive at a view that challenges the canonical portrait of a speaker who is merely "carried away by his own imagination," and a "distraught and essentially morbid, febrile imagination" to boot.[28] That portrait is replaced, or at least radically modified, by the picture of a speaker who seeks the applause of some other, more discerning audience for his skill in bullying his interlocutors and his ability to get away with it; a speaker who flaunts his contempt for his interlocutors by mimicking their reassurances, playing on their expectations of regal conduct, throwing his pusillanimity and despair in their faces, and daring them to reveal rather than suppress their contempt for him. The pleasure he clearly derives, the applause he seeks, and the privileged audience he appeals to must be imagined as sardonic. It is the vertiginous pleasure in self-contempt and in the pursuit of moral self-degradation. This pleasure is increased by his rhetorical command over the scene and course of the self-undoing that will bring him to justice. Since I think the inward observer audits a performance textually depicted as the unfolding of a "spiritual" conflict, a drama of despair, I am not averse to the idea that Richard conducts this drama for the listening pleasure of another observer as well, namely, God.

FIVE

The Fight for the Future Perfect
Richard II, 3.2 (II)

The language-game of reporting can be given such a turn that
a report is not meant to inform the hearer about its subject
matter but about the person making the report.

Ludwig Wittgenstein

The nature of bad news infects the teller.

William Shakespeare

The remainder of 3.2 is organized around Richard's reaction to
the bad news brought by two messengers, the Earl of Salisbury
and someone identified only as Scroope until the following scene,
when Percy dubs him Sir Stephen (3.3.28). Poor Scroope has no
other piece of the play's action, though he is allowed to stand silently on stage during part of 3.3, and perhaps this is his reward
for the canny discretion and careful eloquence with which he delivers his three parcels of information in 3.2: the general shift of
support to Bolingbroke anticipated by the discussion at the end
of 2.2, the deaths of Bushy, Greene, and the Earl of Wiltshire,
sentenced by Bolingbroke in 3.1, and York's desertion, which occurs in 2.3. Salisbury, by contrast, is involved in the news he
brings, having been unable to persuade the Welsh Captain to
keep his troops from abandoning Richard's cause (2.4); and
whereas Scroope fades into nothingness, Salisbury "achieves closure," that is, he is honored at the end of the play by the report of
his decapitation. It turns out that the accuracy of Salisbury's report is open to question,[1] but both he and Scroope use tricks of
the messenger's trade that bend the bad tidings into odd shapes

104

in order to control Richard's reaction not only to the message but also to the messenger.

The clustered reports of events building up since 2.1 accentuate the parlous condition of Richard's regime, but since they refer to what *we* already know, their function is not expository. Nor do they produce any narrative results. Except for 1.2 (which tells us something new about Gaunt), this is the first scene in which the action doesn't move forward. Nothing significant *happens*. But something significant *goes on:* Richard reacts, and his reactions assume a new form which will persist through the remainder of the play. The scene is structured primarily to display those reactions, and the odd thing about this is that Richard's reactions are themselves displays of reaction. He uses the reception of bad news to showcase rhetorically exaggerated postures that alternate, as Coleridge puts it, between "unmanly despair and . . . ungrounded hope."[2] Initially, the scene appears to direct curiosity toward the question "How will he take the news?", but it soon shifts attention to another question, "What lies behind his blatant experiments in self-representation?"

The second question is linked to another peculiarity of the scene. What the messengers report may not be news to us but presumably it is news to Richard. Or is it news? In the apostrophe uttered before the messengers arrive, he shows that someone has told him about rebel cavalry trampling his earth. Though he appears ignorant of particular "facts" relayed by Salisbury and Scroope, the decline in his fortunes can scarcely be a surprise to him since, as we have seen, the downward drift owes much to his mastery of the logistics of self-subversion. If I assume that he has helped set it in motion, I can easily imagine that the inward observer is watching the scenario unfold with a strange mixture of fascination, curiosity, anger, and bitter pleasure and that his displays of reaction are projected from that voyeuristic "coign of vantage." Some of the reported details—the Welsh defection and the execution of his followers—should be surprising, and there are spaces in the script for him to register surprise, but there is very little surprise in his language. This may be tested by a glance at his first reaction.

When Salisbury enters and Richard asks him how far off his power (army) is, the messenger meets the question with a dark little pun and builds up to the bad news with some apocalyptic foreplay:

> Nor near nor farther off, my gracious lord,
> Than this weak arm; discomfort guides my tongue,
> And bids me speak of nothing but despair.
> One day too late, I fear me, noble lord,
> Hath clouded all thy happy days on earth.
> O, call back yesterday, bid time return,
> And thou shalt have twelve thousand fighting men!
> To-day, to-day, unhappy day too late,
> O'erthrows thy joys, friends, fortune and thy state;
> For all the Welshmen, hearing thou wert dead,
> Are gone to Bolingbroke, dispers'd and fled.
>
> (64–74)

This news sounds bad indeed, and Salisbury commends its badness like a salesman promoting his wares: this is the worst possible message; no other message or messenger could match it either in finality or in tuneful despair. Before Richard can show his appreciation, Aumerle breaks in with "Comfort, my liege, why looks your grace so pale?" (75). Reading this as a cue to the king's physical reaction—he blanches, he totters—I am inclined to give Aumerle the benefit of the doubt by assuming that his is not a mere puzzled request for information about the causes of sudden pallor. The question is probably Aumerle's way of urging Richard to take, or at least show, courage regardless of how bad the situation is. And it may be meant to suggest that Salisbury overstates its hopelessness. Richard will have none of this. Aumerle has interrupted the lilting downhill rhythm of the doom Salisbury offers; he has asked the silly question:

> But now the blood of twenty thousand men
> Did triumph in my face, and they are fled;
> And till so much blood thither come again,
> Have I not reason to look pale and dead?
> All souls that will be safe, fly from my side,
> For time hath set a blot upon my pride.
>
> *Aum.* Comfort, my liege, remember who you are.
> *Rich.* I had forgot myself, am I not king?

Awake, thou coward majesty! thou sleepest.
Is not the king's name forty thousand names?
Arm, arm, my name! A puny subject strikes
At thy great glory. Look not to the ground,
Ye favorites of a king, are we not high?
High be our thoughts. I know my uncle York
Hath power enough to serve our turn.

(76–90)

This speaker's discomfiture is not so great as to prevent him from recuperating Salisbury's closing rhymes and launching into a "highly emotional speech . . . in the form of a sestet."[3] Nor is it so great as to prevent him from embarrassing the silly question by devoting a quatrain to political hematology before he turns back to meet Salisbury's challenge with his own closing-time couplet. When Aumerle tries to take the initiative by standing on Richard's dignity, his reminder provokes a dutifully abrupt reversal of field: the king shifts from downward to upward hyperbole and proceeds to remember, if not who he is, then at least what the orthodox ideology tells him he is expected to say he is. The reply is in the antic vein of "God for his Richard hath in heavenly pay," and the inflation of numbers, from twelve to twenty to forty thousand, contributes to this effect.[4] Had he bemoaned the blood loss of no more than Salisbury's original twelve thousand and had he summoned up manpower instead of namepower, Coleridge's assumption that Richard *feels* "unmanly despair" and "ungrounded hope" would be more tenable. Even the Quarto's "twenty thousand names," coupled with our knowledge and Richard's ignorance of York's desertion, would support the idea that ungrounded hope is a feeling, a fantasy, he indulges in. But the effect of a conspicuously sudden and extreme reversal of sentiment is exaggerated by the jump to twenty (excessive despair) and then to forty (excessive hope).

Richard thus solicits mockery both for his lack of courage and for his reliance on the magical namepower which is traditionally included among the benefits that accrue from divine right. Both moves are postures—not feelings but displays of emotion, not indulgence in self-pity and fantasy but representations of indulgence. The final, apparently complacent reference to York's power is, I think, of a piece with this performance and is another instance of the auditory voyeurism I described above. Listening with Aumerle's ears I am mildly gratified to hear Richard casting about for comfort, though as a reader/auditor I know how cold that comfort is. And if I listen with Richard's ears, recalling the mood and circumstances in which he appointed York, I hear a much more sardonic accent beneath the complacency: "power enough to serve our turn" bites hard and deep when we suspect Richard of having accurately assessed the limits of York's power and dependability.

This mordancy indicates that something other than esthetic detachment or theatrical self-indulgence lies behind Richard's displays. There is a feeling of anger whose direction is diffuse. Consider, for example, the ambivalent rhetorical status of "All souls that will be safe, fly from my side, / For time hath set a blot upon my pride." This is either a description of what has already happened or an exhortation to make it happen.[5] In both readings "safe" has negative connotations, but the bitterness runs in different directions. The statement in the indicative mood is, "I am being betrayed and abandoned by all those who would save their own skins when they see their king in trouble." Here anger is directed outward at those who heed the maxim to which Lear's Fool gives classic utterance: "Let go thy hold when a great wheel runs down a hill, lest it break thy neck with following" (2.4.71). In the imperative construction, it is Richard who gives the advice, and although "that will be safe" still glances at the tendency to self-interest the burden of anger is redirected either to time and adversity or to himself for the "pride" that led to his downfall. If we read the second line as moral self-criticism, he could be asking for the abandonment he deserves, but if the line expresses the ill-starred victim's frustrated response to undeserved misfortune, the sentiment conveyed by the couplet is reconfigured to something closer to self-pity. The couplet itself is noncommittal about these options. Its indeterminate mood together with the vagueness of the final metaphor (and of its key terms, "time," "blot," and "pride") sustain the diffuseness of the feeling it articulates. It creates a speaker still uncertain of what he is committing himself to, yet still pushing experimentally forward. But in the context of the sestet, the operatic projection of terminal hopelessness and self-pity prevails over the anger of moral self-criticism. The anger immediately finds a new outlet in the mocking tone with which Richard pretends to satisfy Aumerle's demand that he remember who he is. Even as his inflated fantasy of royal power illustrates the prideful ideology time is sure to blot (and has already blotted), "Look not to the ground" turns the tables on his auditors: "Chin up," their brave leader urges, "don't give up hope." But the implicit stage direction glances at another possibility: "Don't be embarrassed."

This undertone of anger is one of the sharpest impressions Richard's performance leaves me with—anger persisting in or rekindled by the display of operatic emotions. "Bad is the trade that must play the fool to sorrow, / Ang'ring itself and others": Edgar's bitter aside (*King Lear*, 4.1.38–39) describes the relationship between the feeling *in* Richard's language and the emotions displayed *by* it. Etymologically, *feeling* is connected to the touch of the hand, the intimate sense, what the body perceives through contact, whereas *emotion* designates what moves out.[6] This language is in touch with relatively unspecific anger, but it sends out a set of relatively specific emotional postures. Another striking feature of 3.2 is the sense it conveys that Richard is experimentally developing a portfolio of such postures and keying them to familiar themes: not only the "cess of majesty" but also its inalienability, power, and divinity, and then again its lethal effect on its incumbents; the king as thaumaturge, as deputy of God, as figure of the betrayed Christ, as victim of the crown. His "arialike effusions" on these themes, along with those on the consolations of philosophy or religion, are more than exercises in bathetic incantation and thundering fustian.[7] Alternating between postures of excessive hope and excessive despair, they not only play on contradictions in the received ideology but also parody the resources it provides for rationalizing any of the difficulties to which its contradictions give rise.

In this scene, then, Richard fans out for display a variety of emotions that are consistent only in being appropriate to different stages of his downfall—as if he is exploring or rehearsing attitudes he might adopt in the scenes to come—and in the air of mockery that signifies not his detachment but his alienation from all of them. The anger behind the experiment expresses itself in another form of aggression: interlocutory competitiveness. Thus his duel with the messengers continues when Scroope arrives and performs the ritual salute: "More health and happiness betide my liege / Than can my care-tun'd tongue deliver him" (91–92). Schooled by his encounter with Salisbury, Richard accepts this as an invitation to attack and effectually preempts the messenger function with a few flourishes that demonstrate the high standards of woe he challenges Scroope's tidings to meet:

> Mine ear is open and my heart prepar'd.
> The worst is worldly loss thou canst unfold.
> Say, is my kingdom lost? why, 'twas my care,
> And what loss is it to be rid of care?
> Strives Bolingbroke to be as great as we?
> Greater he shall not be. If he serve God,
> We'll serve him too, and be his fellow so.
> Revolt our subjects? that we cannot mend;
> They break their faith to God as well as us.
> Cry woe, destruction, ruin, and decay—
> The worst is death, and death will have his day.
>   (93–103)

Richard now begins to find a way to take advantage of Carlisle's advice and use the heavenly means offered by religion, but it is a use undreamt of in the bishop's philosophy. The religious register is partly for the display of the Higher Resignation, a display which might appeal to any auditors onstage and in the future who share G. L. Kittredge's feeling that Dr. Johnson's words aptly describe this speech: "In his prosperity we saw him imperious and oppressive; but in his distress he is wise, patient, and pious."[8] I don't think Richard himself should be entirely excluded from this audience, and I say this mainly to emphasize the point that although he strikes one pose after another, pious hypocrisy is not his game. Like Richard III, he may seem to enjoy sending it up, but since his scenario is more complex and devious, both his moral and his theatrical pleasures differ from the other Richard's.[9] I agree with Blanpied that in this scene his "postures—in whatever degree sincere or self-indulgent—are experiments, meant to be used up in performance; not hypocrisy, but improvisations" (*Time and the Artist*, 126).

Nevertheless, a shift of auditory perspective isolates a second register in the cloven message. To the auditor(s) within, heaven offers means of another kind: a language that enables him to word and grapple with, perhaps eventually to understand, the spiritual shadowplot of self-despite and self-undoing. In this sardonic register the speech edges toward an explicit summary of the doom-web he weaves for Bolingbroke and himself: they will do God's work together, serve Him as the means by which to bring "succor and redress" to England through the deposing of a wicked king, and He will reward their perfidious service with worse than worldly loss. Richard will sacrifice himself and Bolingbroke for the sake of the crown. According to the moral logic of this shadowplot, it is only by striving to be greater and rising in revolt that the bad king's "puny subject" can serve God, and the catch is that to serve God in this way is simultaneously to break faith with God. Bolingbroke's language in the next two plays will show that he accepts this logic. When he reinvents his relation to Richard by transferring it to his son, he seems motivated by the need to persuade himself that Richard did not deserve to be king, and that although Bolingbroke did not have the right to unking him, much less kill him, he nevertheless heroically sacrificed his own chance for salvation and ran the risk of destroying his reputation for the good of his country. This is precisely the scenario I find compressed in Richard's speech to Scroope. His complicity in it is glanced at in line 99: "We'll serve him too, and be his fellow so." The idea that the crown can be purified, preserved, sent safely beyond Bolingbroke, seems to be taking shape in these lines.[10]

In addition to these forked messages, the speech enacts a more immediate performative function as a rhetorical duel with the messenger. The final couplet has been described as "a vision of universal chaos which is itself a hysterical evasion of the truth";[11] it is in fact, however, neither visionary nor hysterical, but a specific challenge to Scroope. Richard's second sentence (94) minimizes Scroope's response in advance. He defies the puny messenger to be as great as he in crying woe, flashes his spiritual armor, and makes another pass at him in the final couplet. Scroope first parries this thrust—"Glad am I that your Highness is so arm'd / To bear the tidings of calamity" (104–5)—and then circles warily around the armed Highness with a simile whose hard riposte is deferred and prepared for by the fluency of its vehicle:

> Like an unseasonable stormy day,
> Which makes the silver rivers drown their shores,
> As if the world were all dissolv'd to tears,
> So high above his limits swells the rage
> Of Bolingbroke, covering your fearful land
> With hard bright steel, and hearts harder than steel.
>   (106–11)

By itself, the performance of a double analogy, simile within simile, is impressive enough to merit a royal commendation. Even in this atmosphere of ritualized verse, it marks its speaker as a literary exquisite qualified to tilt with kings. I read the addition of the second vehicle, in the third line, as a compensatory act, inflating too small and pastoral an image to the cosmic scale solicited by Richard's challenge. Yet that image of world-purging grief speaks beyond the framework of rhetorical battle to something deeper and more fundamental in the play's community. It speaks of remorse, shame, the desire to be obliterated and made new, the longing for forgiveness. What we have seen, for example, of Gaunt, Mowbray, the Duchess of Gloucester, the Queen, and York suggests their immersion in the conceptual medium of the image. For them Richard seems to provide the focus of the anxiety they acknowledge, the guilt, suspicion, or impotence their language betrays in the face of deeply divided loyalties and the misuse of the royal office protected by divine sanctions. The text of their language conveys a sense of speech conspicuously inhibited and carefully channeled, a sense therefore of things left unsaid, things that had better not be said, things painful even to think. It conveys the sense of a community of speakers who are, in the full archaic and Spenserian amplitude of the term, *sad.* They are the creatures not of an unseasonable day but of a dissolving world. And this changes the meaning of Bolingbroke's rage: delete the image, and he is the cause of tears and fear; include it, and he becomes their effect. The silver rivers of the old world's woe precipitate out the untimely flood of steel and indurate the hearts of Bolingbroke's supporters. The land that weeps and fears for the imminence of the king's downfall and civil strife also weeps and fears because Richard has brought it to this pass.

I think this reading makes more sense of the remainder of Scroope's utterance, which in one respect I find very odd. He goes on to list the four groups of irregulars who rally to Bolingbroke's side:

> White-beards have arm'd their thin and hairless scalps
> Against thy majesty; boys, with women's voices
> Strive to speak big, and clap their female joints
> In stiff unwieldy arms against thy crown;
> Thy very beadsmen learn to bend their bows
> Of double-fatal yew against thy state;
> Yea, distaff-women manage rusty bills
> Against thy seat . . .
>
> (112–19)

This is odd because, whether the list of irregulars is appositional or additional to the phrase denoting hard-hearted bearers of steel, it does not depict a serious *military* challenge. It testifies less to the threat posed by such an army than to the universal disaffection that enables Bolingbroke to mobilize popular support. Thus it decisively changes the meaning of "your fearful land." The motivating cause is focused by the first item in the series, which suggests that the white-beards have been exposed to and are protecting themselves against the predatory acts of "thy majesty"; the remaining incidences of "against" convert the fearful defense into an attack, an attack predicted and indeed encouraged by those who had knowingly alienated the "hateful commons" (2.2.137).[12]

Scroope thus meets Richard's challenge with a reply whose major implication is that the king has empowered the impotent against him and brought woe on himself by the moral irresponsibility of his regime; the willingness to fight of those unfit for warfare testifies to the degree of fear and hate Richard has aroused, and this suggests that Bolingbroke is only a catalyst or focus for that preexisting disaffection. Scroope's message repeats in coded form the substance of Gaunt's earlier recriminations, and it is only one logical step away from the ancient idea that the king, as source of the "Devouring pestilence" that "hangs in our air" (1.3.284), should be driven out and killed. Scroope of course stops well short of this step, but in his concluding couplet he ably signs off with the figure of adynaton, an arch if conventional gesture of inability whose purpose is to indicate that things have been left unsaid: "both young and old rebel / And all goes worse than I have power to tell" (119–20). He may be setting up for the rest of the bad news he possesses, but his coded message as a whole has the broader resonance of a carefully phrased indictment uttered not by a mere messenger but by a troubled subject hinting at what everyone feels. This gives the signoff figure the somewhat different shading of what George Puttenham called "the figure of silence" and classified as an "*auricular* figure of defect": "when we begin to speake a thing, and breake of in the middle way, as if either it needed no further to be spoken of, or that we were ashamed, or afraide to speake it out."[13] Scroope's implication, ceremoniously indirect, is that his riposte to "The worst is worldly loss thou canst unfold" has been moderated to spare his interlocutor.

None of what Richard may be imagined to hear in the speech should surprise the man who had been told in 1.4 that Bolingbroke was wooing the common people, who even then anticipated his return, and who had just said, "All souls that will be safe, fly from my side." Yet it is one thing for *Richard* to say this—whether announcing the news of his plight or urging it as his punishment—and another thing to hear the messenger deliver it not only as news but also as an implied moral indictment: the plight reaffirmed in concrete detail; the bitter wish come true. Taking this into account affects one's reading of the rueful compliment with which he begins his reply: "Too well, too well thou tell'st a tale so ill" (121). The jingling soundplay signifies collectedness rather than hysteria, but the collectedness I hear is cold rather than cool. It is the sound of gathering anger—the anger of justified revenge Richard now (with understandable pleasure) justifiably looks forward to expressing. It animates the gesture of wry civility in line 121 that blunts the force of the messenger's signoff move by praising his manner: Richard reduces the "figure of silence" to an instance of the modesty topos that conventionally asks for such praise. But the effect of the compliment is not so much a slap on the back as a pat on the head, not "Good work!" but "Nice try," as if he expected more matter, bigger and better trouble, to aim his anger at. And he immediately sets out to look for it. Taking his cue from the report of universal disaffection, he shifts the blame for what has happened from himself and prepares to receive the backstab that will justify the conversion of angry self-despite to punitive justice:

> Where is the Earl of Wiltshire? where is Bagot?
> What is become of Bushy? where is Greene?
> That they have let the dangerous enemy
> Measure our confines with such peaceful steps?
> If we prevail, their heads shall pay for it:
> I warrant they have made peace with Bolingbroke.
> (122–27)

Since we know where they are, we are in a good position to appreciate the advantage this gives Scroope and to applaud the disingenuous feint by which he sets up the bellow Richard is clearly ready to let fly:

>   Peace have they made with him indeed, my lord.
> *Rich.*   O villains, vipers, damn'd without redemption![14]
>   Dogs, easily won to fawn on any man!
>   Snakes, in my heart-blood warm'd, that sting my heart!
>   Three Judases, each one thrice worse than Judas!
>   Would they make peace? Terrible hell,
>   Make war upon their spotted souls for this!
> (128–34)

Continuing to try on "The means that heaven yields," he temporarily slips out of the character of Dr. Johnson's "wise, patient, and pious" man of sorrows and into a more energetic version of the Betrayed Christ.[15] "The effect," Traversi writes, "is once more simultaneously one of hysteria, emotional excess, and of true tragedy; of an inadequate king failing to respond to his situation and of the sacred institution of monarchy betrayed in the perverse following of self-interest" (*Shakespeare*, 32). But the effect is primarily another exercise in rhetorical self-degradation, a citational parody in which the role of Christ is enunciated in the accents of Herod. The massed redundancies (of sound, epithets, concepts), the verbal repetitions, the hyperboles, and the sleek antithesis of "make peace"/"Make war" present for his auditors' delectation a fuming pantocrator in the Marlovian mode.

Traversi's reference is to the effect produced by Shakespeare's portrayal of Richard, and it lacks the recursive complement that would enhance its interpretive force: in Shakespeare's portrayal of Richard's portrayal of himself, some of the effects Traversi describes are effects Richard's language seeks to produce by such melodramatic displays of emotion and such conspicuously inadequate responses to the situation as this one. For this is not merely a double-tongued displacement of guilt he knows he shares, converting backroom complicity to the stark opposition between Christ and his oversupply of Judases. It is a *staging* of the displacement. It is of course possible to imagine that this, the first of Richard's two overt appeals to crucifixional fantasy, signifies the formation of a new idea in his scenario of self-undoing, the idea that he is offering himself up as a sacrifice to save the crown—in Northumberland's words, to "Redeem from broking pawn the blemish'd crown" (2.1.293)—from his own grasp and ultimately, perhaps, from Bolingbroke's and that this sacrifice may "win a new world's crown" (5.1.24) when "the king's blood" will have "stain'd the king's own land" (5.5.110). But I don't see how this possibility can be entertained without at the same time acknowledging the bitterness of the accents that allude to the fantasy. Since Richard is well aware that his audience judges him to have betrayed the monarchy "in the perverse following of self-interest," the shift of focus to his own Christlike victimization must be a calculated attempt at outrage whose message is "write me down an ass, or knave, or worse." The Richard I imagine continually pushes his auditors to see how much nonsense he can get away with before they check him and treat him as he deserves. In this respect 3.2 is a kind of rehearsal for his confrontations with Bolingbroke in 3.3 and 4.1 where, from a certain standpoint, he will get away with more than is good for either Bolingbroke or himself.

Having prompted Richard's outburst, the redoubtable Scroope scores his point:

>   Sweet love, I see, changing his property,
>   Turns to the sourest and most deadly hate.
>   Again uncurse their souls; their peace is made
>   With heads and not with hands; those whom you curse
>   Have felt the worst of death's destroying wound,
>   And lie full low, grav'd in the hollow ground.
> *Aum.* Is Bushy, Greene, and the Earl of Wiltshire dead?
> *Scro.* Ay, all of them at Bristow lost their heads.
> *Aum.* Where is the Duke my father with his power?
> *Rich.* No matter where—of comfort no man speak.
>   Let's talk of graves, of worms, and epitaphs,
>   Make dust our paper, and with rainy eyes
>   Write sorrow on the bosom of the earth.
>   Let's choose executors and talk of wills.
>   And yet not so—for what can we bequeath
>   Save our deposed bodies to the ground?
>   Our lands, our lives, and all, are Bolingbroke's,
>   And nothing can we call our own but death;
>   And that small model of the barren earth
>   Which serves as paste and cover to our bones.
>   For God's sake let us sit upon the ground
>   And tell sad stories of the death of kings . . .
>
>   (135–56)

Aumerle's interjections open up an interpretive space within which to wonder how Richard reacts before he speaks. Does the bad news shock him into a moment of silence? Does the messenger's rebuke stab him with shame at his ungenerous surmise? Would he have preferred to hear (and have others hear) that his followers had betrayed him? Is the proof of his suspicious and ungenerous nature perversely satisfying to him? Is its expression, its exposure to others, another bid for their contempt? Nothing Richard says throws any light on these questions, thus any attempt to answer them can't be based on the local dramaturgy of this scene; it can only derive from the more synoptic hypothesis we construct about Richard's language and motivation. A conventional psychological reading of his response is easy enough: his shock and grief are denoted by evasive generalization; the speech softens the blow, calls for a good cry, and provides the "comfort" it forbids with the kind of meditation on mortality appropriate to the burial service. Dismissing Aumerle's second question flags the impropriety of so practical a consideration at this moment.

Yet I don't think this reading carries us very far. First, it fails to account for the competitive energy of the speech considered as a response both to the bad news Scroope delivers and to the advantage he gained by the deceptive maneuver enabling him to put Richard momentarily off his guard. Richard dismisses Aumerle's question partly to finish his exchange with the messenger and regain the offensive: "Let's *really* talk of graves. Everyone has to die some time, and for many of us Bolingbroke, like death, is the great equalizer. But surely kings have it worse than others and deserve more tears than their counselors, so let Bushy and company rest in peace and let's turn instead to hear sad stories about the fall of such truly illustrious personages as myself." If I over-emphasize the tartness of the message it is to reiterate the point that Richard is not merely engaged in solipsistic surrender to his fantasies, and the related point that he is not the victim of a self-indulgent author unable to resist the temptation to sacrifice his character on the golden altar of the setpiece. I shall return to this topic after exploring the second and more significant aspect of Richard's response that the conventional reading ignores.

That reading does not explain why Richard concentrates on a particular phrase in Scroope's speech and draws it out in a complex figure. "Grav'd in the hollow ground" triggers the play on engraving and writing, which extends into talk of wills and bequeathal, and beyond that into stories. The repetitions of "our" modulate its reference from the present company of weepers to all humankind, but at the same time there is a swerve back through the mention of "deposed bodies" and Bolingbroke toward the referent of the royal plural.[16] When Richard proposes inscribing and sprinkling the dry earth with sorrow—sorrow that will be preserved like a text—he could still be delivering a eulogy for the lately departed counselors, but when he dismisses the idea of choosing executors Bushy and company begin to fade out of the picture. The distanced meditation on the death of the counselors becomes a prologue to, a model of, the distanced meditation on his own death.

The rhetorical turning point, the moment in which the metaphor of writing begins to pay off, occurs at "And nothing can we call our own but death." That seems like the nadir, but it is the turn toward new life, a new idea of life, and Richard might say, with Northumberland, that "even through the hollow eyes of death / I see life peering" (2.1.270–71). For to call one's death one's own is indeed *something*. It is Gaunt's project, and the Duchess of Gloucester's, and Mowbray's. The aim of the ars moriendi, which may be cultivated at any time in life, is to write one's own epitaph, to shape the death mask that will control the future by representing the deceased as he or she wishes to be remembered. It is an act of autobiography, of autothanatography. The ability to die "our own . . . death" is contingent on disembodiment. The captive casts off "his chains of bondage," deposes "to the ground" the bodily image of the life he has made and wishes to flee from, buries the visible identity that was the target of *appeal*, replaces it with the commemorative icon. So Richard, after glancing at the consumability of fleshly "paste," proposes a gesture that signifies both the return to earth ("let us sit upon the ground") and the concealment of the buried life by the act of autothanatography ("tell sad stories of the death of kings").

Having identified the literary genre to which his story will belong, he proceeds to insinuate his chapter into the collection during a brief survey of the variety of regicidal possibilities:

> How some have been depos'd, some slain in war,
> Some haunted by the ghosts they have deposed,
> Some poisoned by their wives, some sleeping kill'd,
> All murthered . . .
>
> (157–60)

He lists his preferential category first but considerately reserves space for Bolingbroke and in fact features the category he assigns him to by allocating a whole line to it (158). The logic of the motif that controls the passage ("All murthered") gives the line and its speaker a sinister reach: "Some haunted [to death] by the ghosts they have deposed." Richard's posthumous revenge, yoking Bolingbroke's fate to his own, is foreshadowed in the phrase construction: the two categories are yoked together and distinguished from the others by the repetition of the key word and of the unabridged present perfect form ("have been depos'd," "have deposed"). This tense is tinged with a progressive aspect that specifies a more open and indefinite relation of past to present, as a contrast with the closure of the simple preterit will show: "some were depos'd, some slain in war, / Some haunted by the ghosts that they deposed, / Some poison'd by their wives, some sleeping kill'd, / All murthered." Since "deposed" and "haunted" lack the finality of "slain," "poisoned," and "kill'd," the present perfect emphasizes uncompleted action, persistent effects that can spread over time and even float into the future.[17] As Benveniste argues, the present perfect "creates a living connection between the past event and the present" of the speaker "who relates the facts as a witness, as a participant." Indeed, the class of compound tenses called "perfect" indicates a form of "anteriority" that "does not carry any reference to time by itself" and is always determined "with respect to the correlative simple tense. It creates a logical and intralinguistic connection and does not reflect a chronological one."[18]

In our passage, the simple tense is the hortatory present subjunctive, "let us . . . tell," whose object, "sad stories," specifies a loose and ambiguous relation to history, since what are to be recounted are not events themselves but previous accounts, and these may be parabolic, exemplary, false, or fictive, as well as historical. Insofar as they are exemplary or representative they are repeatable and generic: Richard's "How" is misleading because it promises stories he doesn't tell; the word should be "That," for the series of clauses *are* the stories, and they have the status of open categories. A strange irony is produced by the fact that the examples recall the later events dramatized in the earlier tetralogy. Bolingbroke's sad story, for example, falls in the same category as that of his theatrical precursor and historical postcursor, Richard III. If this is an allusion it can only be Shakespeare's (not Richard's), that is, it can only be an effect of the text that conveys information about its speaker's motivation. What I think it shows is that Richard's project is to convert past and present fictions into future history.[19] The chronological openness of the present perfect, along with its subordination to the speaker's present, enables Richard to draw it into negotiations with the future perfect.

It is an easy glide from "some have been depos'd" through "some will be depos'd" to "some will have been depos'd," and I think the future perfect tense denotes Richard's real destination—the destination not merely of the stories he *tells* but of the story he *performs* by telling sad stories, the story of Richard he fashions in all his public speeches from 2.2 on. In psychoanalysis the future perfect is the tense of *undoing*, not only the pathological negation of the past Freud isolated as an obsessional symptom (*Ungeschehenmachen*) but also its homeopathic antidote, the undoing that occurs during the process of analysis ("If I believe this story, then I will have been other than I was, or thought I was").[20] Here the reference is to the past rather than to the future, but the resemblance in structure suggests that the desire of undoing may be inextricably intertwined with the more positive impulses to autothanatography. The future perfect is at any rate its operative tense, because it governs the mediated transactions between correspondents separated from each other by space and time.[21] A good model of Richard's strategy is provided by the epistolary formula "By the time you receive this letter, I will have been . . ." His public speeches display the postures, enact the roles, develop the portfolio that composes into the message he sends posterity. And his sad story will be all the more readily grasped and accepted for following well-established precedents, "such traditional works as the *Fall of Princes*, the *Mirror for Magistrates*, and the *Monk's Tale*. . . . The 'moral' is fully traditional."[22]

Death by crowning is the motif Richard selects for the story of his demise with which he now sets out to regale his audience. The reason kings get murdered is that

> within the hollow crown
> That rounds the mortal temples of a king
> Keeps Death his court, and there the antic sits,
> Scoffing his state and grinning at his pomp,

> Allowing him a breath, a little scene,
> To monarchize, be fear'd, and kill with looks;
> Infusing him with self and vain conceit,
> As if this flesh which walls about our life
> Were brass impregnable; and, humor'd thus,
> Comes at the last, and with a little pin
> Bores through his castle wall, and farewell king!
>
> (160–70)

In context, this feints toward generalized application of the *vanitas* theme to the sad lot of kings: "The crown is a deadly dangerous office; all kings are victims; I am an instance of the general case."[23] The familiarity of the emblem adds to its generalizing force. "This particular application of the play metaphor to the king," Anne Barton writes, "is essentially medieval. It is allied to the bitter revelry of the Dance of Death, to a general recognition of the world's vanity, the necessity of practising the *ars moriendi*."[24]

The message is given particularity and bite by its echo of the following lines from Gaunt's diatribe:

> A thousand flatterers sit within thy crown,
> Whose compass is no bigger than thy head,
> And yet, incaged in so small a verge,
> The waste is no whit lesser than thy land.
>
> (2.1.100–103)

The first two lines conflate the flatterers protected by the power of the crown with their influence on Richard's mind, and the chief representatives of this influential faction, as Bolingbroke makes clear in 3.1, were the recently executed counselors. In Richard's emblem, Death personifies the flatterers who encouraged his wasteful folly and made him *their* allowed fool. The echo tempts me to wonder, just for a moment, whether Richard is experimenting with a rationalization, namely, that those flatterers were courtiers of Death and received their proper punishment; that the folly that cost them their lives will soon cost him his; and that this will be his punishment, the crown's revenge on its unworthy possessor. According to this logic, by not betraying Richard, Bushy and company remained complicit with him in the mortal folly that betrayed England. What atonement would be more appropriate than to design the murder he anticipates as a purifying sacrifice, an act of martyrdom that will stain both the conscience and the regime of his Lancastrian Pilate? "Exton, thy fierce hand / Hath with the king's blood stain'd the king's own land. / Mount, mount, my soul!" Lois Potter has astutely observed the difference between Richard as the "ritualistic King of Sorrows" and "the other Richard: sharp-tongued, self-mocking and quite unresigned," at best "unsure of his own salvation" and viewing death "not as the way to 'a new world's crown' but as 'being nothing.'" Her contrast illuminates the political imagination and realism of the scenario that culminates in his final speech: "The formality of that speech, and its rhyming couplets, are taken up at once by Exton, establishing the simplified, symbolic view of Richard . . . which is to prevail in the final scene."[25] There the sad legend Richard concocts loses whatever fictiveness it may have had for him ("Mount, mount, my soul! *thy* seat is up on high" dissociates the soul from the speaker and identifies him with his "gross flesh") to become the effectual reality that permanently blights Henry's regime.

If such a design is beginning to take shape in this scene, it is not something Richard shares with his interlocutors. The message for them is that "death is present not only as an external threat of disaster but as the inner inevitability."[26] The conceptual stereotype he promotes is the one that will reappear in various forms in *2 Henry IV* and *Henry V*: the crown is the king's murderer; the king's "hard condition" is to drink "poison'd flattery" while bearing all his subjects' cares and sins and thus suffering "more / Of mortal griefs" than they do. He has discovered that beneath the robes of "thrice-gorgeous ceremony" his flesh is not "impregnable"; indeed, "his castle wall" is paper-thin. It is understandable that when this brittle icon of self-pity is isolated from its interlocutory context it provides more evidence for the idea that Richard is the victim of "manic/depressive leaps" in this scene, or that he is brooding in "metaphysical style . . . on his own mortality," or that he is dwelling "on his tragedy" and "exacting from his plight a sad refinement of sensation."[27] But there are several reasons—rhetorical, syntactical, interlocutory—why these opinions are inadequate.

Consider first the wry phrasing and the plethora of dainty devices—assonance, parallelism, doublets, polysyndeton, the tricolon in line 165, the hendiadys in 166—with which the speaker tangs his description and draws it out slowly in a series of short clauses. The icon of self-pity is not merely being adorned by a depressed and brooding worshiper. It is being served up with brio. And the conclusion, in which he tries on the stereotype, bristles with rhetorical self-confidence:

> Cover your heads, and mock not flesh and blood
> With solemn reverence; throw away respect,
> Tradition, form, and ceremonious duty;
> For you have but mistook me all this while.
> I live with bread like you, feel want,
> Taste grief, need friends—subjected thus,
> How can you say to me, I am a king?
>
> (171–77)

This self-humbling call for fellow feeling is delivered imperiously. It begins, literally, with imperatives, and Baxter, who notes that Richard is "monarchizing" here, admirably catches his double-tongued tone: " 'To monarchize' means, at least in part, to posture as a monarch, to attitudinize. To attitudinize is to adopt an attitude (usually in the interest of exciting admiration for one's own person)"—admiration or, as the repetition of "mock not" implies, vexed embarrassment. The words "solemn reverence," Baxter continues, "call attention to themselves because, while Richard succeeds in dismissing reverence, he does not succeed in banishing solemnity. What could be more solemn than his whole speech, and particularly the last part?" I think the second clause means that it is Baxter and the theater audience who can't work up much reverence for Richard, because he goes on to complain that although Richard's "attempt to ponder seriously the nature of his predicament is commendable, his embrace of his own vulnerable mortality as the absolute truth is, finally, only one more way of succumbing to the vice of attitudinizing."[28]

For Baxter this failure is in the last analysis Shakespeare's, the result of his imperfect tempering of the golden by the moral style. But if we shift from Baxter's perspective to mine—from Shakespeare to Richard and from the theater audience to the onstage audience—his critical response to the speech provides an accurate model of the kind of reaction Richard's language seems intended to provoke: "Watch me succumb once more to the vice of attitudinizing." "I wish he would stop attitudinizing; it's vicious, and kings shouldn't succumb to it; I'm finding it harder and harder every minute to accord his majesty the solemn reverence, the respect and ceremonious duty, his high office commands." If Richard's "mock not" embarrasses his auditors by telling them not to do something they aren't doing, it is plausible to treat it as a calculated effect. The same effect is produced by the studied mock-condescension of "For you have but mistook me all this while"—"I'm only human after all, not the god on earth you took me for." The speech is less a metaphysical reflection than an antic broadcast from within the hollow crown.

Second, in addition to this "attitudinizing" rhetoric, there are syntactical ambiguities in the memento mori section that liberate the meaning of Death from the emblematic enclosure, the conceptual stereotype, within which Richard introduced it. If, for example, he begins by attributing the death of kings to dangers inherent in the office, his handling of the emblem soon confuses the identity and seat of danger's cause. Is Death both king and jester?—a lord of misrule? "*His* court" is presumably Death's rather than the king's, but "his state" and "his pomp" are more ambiguous and permit a momentary fusion. "*Allowing* him . . . a little scene" applies as well to the antic as to the king, and in the next line the jester king becomes Death's mimic. By this time we may be prompted to ask whether Death keeps his court not only within the crown but also within the king's mortal temples. When the two figures are again conflated in the indefinite reference of "humor'd thus," it becomes unclear whether Death bores from without or within: if the former, the king is undone by alien forces impinging from the ambience of the royal court and office; if the latter, the alien inhabits the walled-in life and the king undoes himself. The former message confirms the stereotype of the royal victim and supports the subsequent plea for sympathy. But the latter message identifies the antic with the king and sends another meaning "through the hollow eyes of death": the death alive within him, the death that drives this performance and feeds his self-contempt, is his desire to die and be punished, his fear of that desire, and his desire to go on tasting the fear by bringing on his downfall. Hearing or eliciting this message, gathering it in from my sense of Richard's scenario as a whole, I find the phrases describing his subjection profoundly and poignantly true—"feel want, / Taste grief, need friends"—all the more so inasmuch as their rhetorical context imprisons them in the mockery of a speaker who positively enjoys exhaling the breath of kings, making a little scene, killing himself with words, and trying in general to prove that the ruin he looks forward to is inescapable; a speaker who, moreover, displays his enjoyment to his auditors like an antic grinning at his own pomp and inviting them to scoff at his state.

The rhetorical and interlocutory context provides the third reason in support of the premise that Richard is doing more than catering to a voracious appetite for self-pity. In his exchanges with Scroope and the others he fully engages his interlocutors, competes with them, inflicts fantasies and setpieces on them, and listens to them listen. How much of this they fail to hear is indicated by the one serious response to the speech. Carlisle registers only the stereotype of self-pity and unmanly fear:

> My lord, wise men ne'er sit and wail their woes,
> But presently prevent the ways to wail.
> To fear the foe, since fear oppresseth strength,
> Gives in your weakness strength unto your foe,
> And so your follies fight against yourself.
> Fear and be slain—no worse can come to fight;
> And fight and die is death destroying death,
> Where fearing dying pays death servile breath.

Aum. My father hath a power; inquire of him,
> And learn to make a body of a limb.

Rich. Thou chid'st me well. Proud Bolingbroke, I come
> To change blows with thee for our day of doom.
> This ague fit of fear is overblown;
> An easy task it is to win our own.
> Say, Scroope, where lies our uncle with his power?
> Speak sweetly, man, although thy looks be sour.
>
> (178–93)

Once again the Bishop lectures the wayward king but seems persuaded by what he has seen and heard that heaven's means are not likely to be embraced with enough enthusiasm to turn the tide: his "emphasis is rather on the acceptance of death than on any true reason for hope" and, Traversi adds, this offers "self-deceiving comfort" rather than "true encouragement" (*Shakespeare*, 33). Herford thought that Carlisle's penultimate line "contains the thought . . . that the valorous Soul is emancipated from death" (Variorum, 201), but, as Traversi's comment suggests, the passage seems to advise emancipation *by* death and *from* life through a competent execution of the ars moriendi that will at least entitle Richard to qualify for a version of Malcolm's faint praise, "Nothing became his life / Like the leaving it."

Carlisle states in more somber terms the hero's appeal to the solace of tragic relief first given golden expression by Mowbray in his "Never did captive with a freer heart" aria (1.3.88–96). Richard will appreciate the ideological value of this exit strategy when he confronts Exton, but for the time being it is clearly not high on his list of priorities. Traversi's remark that the advice "fits the mood in Richard against which it seeks to react" (*Shakespeare*, 33) is open to a perverse construal by anyone who suspects Richard of thinking the advice ludicrous, for the Bishop's words describe his scenario: Richard *is* preparing to give strength unto his foe, to arm his follies against himself, and to design a death that will oppress the usurper's strength with fear and ghostly haunting. If no worse can come to fight than "Fear and be slain," that is not bad enough, not insidious enough, to satisfy his taste for the experience in spiritual damnation he plans to perform on Bolingbroke's behalf as well as his own. Thus Richard's rejoinder is an operatic sestet which, in my view, mimics the response he hears Carlisle asking for, stages what Traversi rightly calls "a facile recovery" (33), and prepares the way for its collapse with the question about York suggested by Aumerle.

I imagine that Richard knows the kind of answer to expect before observing Scroope's expression and that the question is wickedly aimed to set up his "equally facile plunge into despair" (Traversi, 33). The Variorum records an audience reaction to

Richard's final line ("Speak sweetly . . .") which I herewith submit in support of this allegation:

> Miss Webster relates that at an early performance of their revival of *Richard II*, the delivery of this line by Maurice Evans drew a wholly unexpected burst of appreciative laughter from the audience. He treasured the line thereafter and it came to be known among the company as "Richard's laugh."   (202)

The discovery of a potential chuckle in a script where few people have found much to laugh at—or laugh with—until the fourth act is cause for more than rejoicing; it is cause for interpretive scrutiny. Assuming that it was Evans's Richard and not Evans himself who should get credit for the laugh, what textual resources could have made it possible? Was it only a local laugh touched off by the antithesis between sweet speech and sour looks? Or do its causes spread out into the environing interlocutory terrain?

I might laugh, for example, if I have been taking note of Richard's verbal contest with the messenger. Scroope introduced the antithesis in rebuking Richard ("Sweet love" vs. "sourest . . . hate," 135), and for me the echo sharpens the tone of demand: Richard is once again crowding poor Scroope, prodding him for more bad news, and inviting him to put on another little messenger show. My amusement would be partly anticipatory: what similes, what literary clichés, what rhetorical detours will Scroope brandish to parade his competence in the art? Listening with Scroope's ears, I hear "Speak sweetly, man" as a request for messengerial self-display, and so I am moved to put the answer, and especially its opening quatrain, in quotation marks, framing it as a sample of prefatory sweetness offered up in the spirit of "How like you this?":

> Men judge by the complexion of the sky
> The state and inclination of the day;
> So may you by my dull and heavy eye:
> My tongue hath but a heavier tale to say.
> I play the torturer by small and small
> To lengthen out the worst that must be spoken:
>   (194–99)

By now we recognize the disease of histrionic self-characterization that afflicts the Ricardian community, and we (or some of us) anticipate a message whose copiousness will match that of Scroope's windup. But no sooner does he prepare to execute his amplificatio than Richard cuts into it:

> Your uncle York is join'd with Bolingbroke,
> And all your northern castles yielded up,
> And all your southern gentlemen in arms
> Upon his party.
> Rich.   Thou hast said enough.
> Beshrew thee, cousin, which didst lead me forth
> Of that sweet way I was in to despair!
> What say you now? What comfort have we now?
> By heaven, I'll hate him everlastingly
> That bids me be of comfort any more.
> (200–208)

The messenger has had his day in the sun and performed his function, which was to provide Richard with a foil that would set off the development of his portfolio and the serial publication of his sad story. "Thou hast said enough": "A heavy blow! I can't take any more of this," but also "We get the point; you've served our turn and are dismissed." Without even a concluding couplet.

I think Richard's laugh is produced by the tension between these two levels of dramatic and interlocutory action, the former mediated through the latter, and by the way the self-preferring presence of interlocutory action aggressively interferes with and upstages the dramatic plot it is putatively supposed to unfold. From the conventional standpoint, this approaches a means-end reversal the effect of which is to center our attention on the immediate texture and interplay of speech acts as the figure for which the larger pattern of the historical tragedy provides the ground. The complex acts of auditory imagination called forth by this centering open up within the historical drama the spiritual drama I have been referring to as Richard's scenario. It is the perspective from within the mortal temples of the king—the perspective on both the historical drama and the interlocutory action—that I think accounts for Richard's laugh.

In Margaret Webster's report "Richard's laugh" is meant as

an objective genitive, but I propose shifting it to a subjective genitive in order to correlate the audience response with the character's black-humored amusement. According to the procedure I outlined in the last chapter, this enables us to take note of the audience response in order to convert it to a cue to the audition going on within the speaker. Thus, for example, when Richard apostrophizes Bolingbroke for Carlisle's benefit, promises to "change blows with thee," and then asserts that "This ague fit of fear is overblown," I detect the antic's grin behind the pomp of "blows" and "overblown," hearing "bluster" in the first and "inflated" in the second. The impression that he is sending up both Carlisle's simplistic proposal and his own attitudinizing affects my response to "Say, Scroope, where lies our uncle with his power?", especially if I assume that news of York's defection would not surprise him. For then I am inclined to think that he is enlisting the help of the artful bringer of bad tidings to send up Aumerle as well: "Make a body of a limb indeed! Come, sourfaced Scroope, let's sweetly disabuse Aumerle. . . . *Q.E.D.*: Cousin, what say you now?" His immediate relish in forked speech, his masterful orchestration of these effects, and his firm grip on the progress of his autothanatography: these, and not merely a casual antithesis, generate the inner laughter resonated by the signifying echo of Maurice Evans's audience.

Richard's expostulation against comfort is a last tug at the stitches of a minor conflict threading through the scene. It began when he prefaced his "searching eye of heaven" extravaganza with "Discomfortable cousin" (36), which was a response to Aumerle's charge that "we are too remiss" in neglecting the means offered by heaven. It continued with Aumerle's two entreaties to comfort in the Salisbury exchange (75, 82) and with Richard's dismissal of Aumerle's first inquiry into his father's whereabouts (143), "No matter where—of comfort no man speak" (144). The comfort Aumerle and Carlisle urge on him is what he rejects—what he has been rejecting—as flattery: the hope that all may not yet be lost and, as a backup comfort, the prospect of tragic relief in making a last stand, fighting to the death, going out in style. He chooses instead an equally operatic alternative, conclusively dressed up in the couplets that end the scene:

> Go to Flint Castle, there I'll pine away—
> A king, woe's slave, shall kingly woe obey.
> That power I have, discharge, and let them go
> To ear the land that hath some hope to grow,
> For I have none. Let no man speak again
> To alter this, for counsel is but vain.

Aum. My liege, one word.

Rich.   He does me double wrong
> That wounds me with the flatteries of his tongue.
> Discharge my followers; let them hence away,
> From Richard's night, to Bolingbroke's fair day.
>   (209–18)

Lines 211–13 repeat, in more unambiguously hortatory form, the sentiment occasioned earlier by Salisbury's news, "All souls that will be safe, fly from my side" (80), and the rationale behind the order is borrowed from the stereotypical reading of the *vanitas* emblem: he has no hope because, *qua king,* he is a generic victim of the office, and to try to persuade him otherwise is flattery.

Richard's tale of "kingly woe" is the sweet way to despair which he claims to fancy more than the flattering path to comfort proposed by Carlisle and Aumerle. Against their invitation to tragic relief he recommends pathetic relief: he will resign himself to his fate, vanish into the silent woodwork of Flint Castle far from the wounding tongues and ears of his kingdom—from all, that is, except his own. A nice touch of royal privilege, of lonely pride, appears in the contrast between his monopoly on kingly woe and the industrious husbandry to which he consigns those who hope to grow: the play on "To ear" extends the social category of peasant or yeoman from discharged soldiers to more ambitious pursuants of power, whom he urges to cultivate the nation's ears. But can despondent men play so nicely with their words? Richard's language makes me suspect his commitment to the sweet way. He does not say he "*must* obey kingly woe"; he says he "*shall* obey" it, and the willfulness signaled by the imperative implies that he *abjures* hope, not simply that there *is* no hope. Nor is he content merely to be abandoned by his followers, which, according to the messengers' bad news, is all but a fait accompli. Refusing to be bullied by either the news or the messengers, he takes over responsibility for finishing the task: if the king is to be abandoned it will be by royal fiat.

This move extends suspicion to the final couplet, which trips too tunefully through the image that foredooms his benighted fall by naturalizing it. Thus he does not seem to *embrace* his surrender to the sweet way. Rather, he seems to *display* it, and to display it as another fantasy, in language that offers a glimpse of a different—a far more bitter—way to despair. For if we listen to these lines with Richard's ears, the sweet fantasy itself takes on the aspect of flattery, of false consolation. It is the consolation, as Dr. Johnson put it, of "a mind convinced that his distress is without a remedy, and preparing to submit quietly to irresistible calamity" (Variorum, 204). Were Richard to entertain that conviction, he would do himself a double wrong. Not only would he deceive himself into embracing the victim's role he performs for others, he would also deprive himself of the remedy he has the power and will to dispense, the bitter remedy he will decoct in "Here, cousin, seize the crown." The self-mockery that edges all his charades in this scene signifies his dedication to the bitter way, the way leading to the "sour cross" of 4.1. If he is to "taste grief" it will be on his own terms, and those terms are more deeply political, more darkly spiritual than the fantasies of escape offered by the golden way of tragic relief and the sweet way of pathetic relief.

But why shouldn't the golden way be attractive to him? Supposing the Ricardian scenario I have been developing to be even faintly plausible, how could the chance to go out in style frustrate his desire to undo himself? Wouldn't a rousing Hotspurious finish at the Battle of Flint Castle embellish his autothanatography? I ask these questions partly to meet a possible objection and partly to suggest that as an interpretive hypothesis the scenario has a logic that imposes constraints on the kinds of sense we make of the passages it throws into evidentiary prominence. We could say, for example, that the alternative of tragic relief would shorten the bitter pleasure of self-despite, would keep Richard from drawing it out and savoring it to the full. We could say further that although going out in style might well deceive others, its danger is that it could deceive him too, and at the moment of truth when he could least afford to succumb to delusion. We could even say that for Richard to remain undeluded, to maintain the voyeur's advantage in promoting discrepant awarenesses, to keep a steady focus on the self-contempt which feeds his contempt for others, he must invent and die his own death. To remain true to one's self-contempt, to mock the postures that would falsify it, bespeaks a certain self-respect which, in Richard's case, extends to pride in his mastery of the politics of self-undoing. Neither tragic nor pathetic relief, neither golden death nor sweet despair would guarantee him the control over his downfall that would enable him sooner or later to take Bolingbroke down with him. His mockery and mimicry are signs of an anger that will not be soothed by the flattering prospect of dying in battle and becoming a heroic underdog dethroned by force and death. The dying lion's rage—here I borrow and freely vary the terms of the Queen's speech at 5.1.26—can be soothed only by the moral logic and power of the gift that will enable him to thrust "forth his paw" into Bolingbroke's heart: "Here, cousin, seize the crown." Richard is preparing to give, not merely to lose, the crown, and for the gift to work its poison he will have to ghostwrite as well as perform the sad tale of deposition and murder by which he will haunt Bolingbroke to death.

These, then, are the pleasures of the bitter way to despair to the course of which Richard begins to give more definite shape in 3.2, a scene that, as I have tried to show, serves as a staging ground, a preparatory sparring session, for the public confrontations in 3.3 and 4.1. The portfolio of poses, the fantasies of tragic and pathetic relief, the little scenes and stations that mark the sweet way to despair are the rhetorical surface of the bitter way, and by "rhetorical" I mean *performative*. This is the surface that Georges Bonnard, in the passage cited early in the last chapter, depicted as a histrionic parade of "elaborate attitudes," "premeditated" and "insincere." We can now see that these need not indicate merely Richard's "absence of character" and "incompetence as a ruler." Bonnard's terms adumbrate a different source and explanation of the parade. First, it could be said that insincerity is itself an effect: Richard stages his emotions and fantasies—of sorrow, self-pity, confidence, resignation, righteous indignation, and despair—with such flamboyance as to make them seem less than convincing. Second, he stages them in traditional and stereotypical form. From this I deduce that they are being put on display as culturally constructed rationalizations.

In Richard's performance of ready-made emotions, the mode of rationalization he targets is the resort to magic. This is most obvious in the thaumaturgical parody of the first two speeches, the fairy magic of the "Dear earth" apostrophe and the spiritual magic of the sun king's searching eye. But in a less obvious manner all his speeches dramatize what may be called a magical view of the world. It is magical in the specific sense given the term by Sartre in his *esquisse* of a phenomenological approach to the emotions, and some of Sartre's comments throw light on what I take to be the object of Richard's parody. He calls emotion "an abrupt drop of consciousness into the magical. Or, if one prefers, there is emotion when the world of instruments abruptly vanishes and the magical world appears in its place."[29] An emotion

> is a transformation of the world. When the paths traced out become too difficult, or when we see no path, we can no longer live in so urgent and difficult a world. All the ways are barred. However, we must act. So we try to change the world, that is, to live as if the connection between things and their potentialities were not ruled by deterministic processes but by magic. Let it be clearly understood that this is not a game; we are driven against a wall, and we throw ourselves into this new attitude with all the strength we can muster. (58–59)

> Thus the origin of emotion is a spontaneous and lived degradation of consciousness in the face of the world. What it cannot endure in one way it tries to grasp in another by going to sleep, by approaching the consciousness of sleep, dream, and hysteria.
>
> (77)

Or, we could add, by creating magical worlds of natural and spiritual sympathy, hierarchies and correspondences, divine and deadly kingships, rituals of tragic and pathetic relief. Sartre's "degradation of consciousness" suggests that emotion is a prototype of the concept of *mauvaise foi*.[30] Like Richard, he "reads with suspicion," and his account of the emotion of "active sadness" speaks directly to a rationalization Richard is especially fond of subjecting to mimicry:

> There is magical exaggeration of the difficulties of the world. Thus, the world . . . appears as unjust and hostile, because it demands *too much* of us, that is, more than it is humanly possible to give. The emotion of active sadness in this case is therefore a magical comedy of impotence; the sick person resembles servants who, having brought thieves into their master's home, have themselves tied up so that it can be clearly seen that they could not have prevented the theft. Only, here, the sick person is tied up by himself and by a thousand tenuous bonds. (67)

This account of active sadness perfectly fits York's behavior in going neuter and pleading his age while bringing the thief Bolingbroke into his master's home. Active sadness, which lies behind the resort of the old to the ars moriendi, can produce a magical world that justifies the nonresponsibility of Gaunt's "God's is the quarrel" and makes possible the "magical comedy" Richard plays in dramatizing his inability to prevent the theft of the crown. The emotions he stages are those that perpetuate—and are privileged by—the royal, religious, and chivalric rituals of a sacramental world. In act 1 Richard presses on Gaunt's resort to the comedy of impotence, and in 2.1 his appointment of York as lord governor may well be a test to see whether York will set the word against the word and violate his own lecture to Richard about lawful succession.

Richard's staging of the comedy in 3.2 is ambivalent because he is experimentally both separating himself from the magical world and establishing his autothanatographic return to it in the future perfect. Whether or not we imagine him to be nostalgic for that world, his performance has the effect of restoring it to attention and viewing it afresh through his parodic mimicry of Bishop-talk. This is, as we know, the effect of *defamiliarization,* the concept Brecht adapted from Shklovskii and advocated as a dramaturgical strategy. I conclude by applying to Richard some of Brecht's remarks in "Alienation Effects in Chinese Acting," the essay in which he first explored the concept. He notes that when the Chinese actor "expresses his awareness of being watched" and also conspicuously "observes himself" while performing, his "object is to appear strange and even surprising to the audience. He achieves this by looking strangely at himself and his work." In the expression of emotions the alienation effect

> intervenes . . . in the form of emotions which need not correspond to those of the character portrayed. On seeing worry the spectator may feel a sensation of joy; on seeing anger, one of disgust. When we speak of exhibiting the outer signs of emotion we do not mean such an exhibition and such a choice of signs that the emotional transference does in fact take place because the actor has managed to infect himself with the emotions portrayed, by exhibiting the outer signs; thus, by letting his voice rise, holding his breath and tightening his neck muscles so that the blood shoots to his head, the actor can easily conjure up a rage. In such a case of course the effect does not occur. But it does occur if the actor at a particular point unexpectedly shows a completely white face, which he has produced mechanically by holding his face in his hands with some white make-up on them.[31]

In a Brechtian production of *Richard II* this might precede Aumerle's "Comfort, my liege, why looks your grace so pale," though I don't recommend it. What I do recommend is shifting Brecht's discussion from actor to character. It is Richard who "expresses his awareness of being watched" and whose object is "to appear strange and even surprising" to the stage audience. Speaking of the actor Charles Laughton playing Galileo, Brecht affirms the principle "that the actor appears on the stage in a double role, . . . that the showman Laughton does not disappear in the Galileo whom he is showing" but "is actually there, standing on the stage and showing us what he imagines Galileo to have been" (194). Similarly the showman Richard shows us what he imagines "Richard" will have become if his performances "take," if the sad story he tells will be the one engraved in the chronicle of kings. Porter's observation that Richard "conceives of even his own actions as if they stood outside time like events in a story" accords with this idea:[32] Richard alienating "Richard" from himself as he alienates the crown and its magical world, deposing himself in "active sadness" from the office of which he is unworthy, and thereby preserving the sanctity of the office. The

"Richard" Richard will have become is the king who sacrificed himself for the crown and who was its victim: Saint Richard the holy martyr, betrayed, abandoned, and crucified, courageous in defeat, a warrior for Christ. My Richard, in short, is a Slit-eyed Analyst who reads his text with suspicion. He keeps one eye on the future perfect tense that has the power to undo the Richard he knows he is and to impose the Richard he performs on all the generations of Wide-eyed Playgoers whose first grandfather is the second king of the Henriad.

EPILOGUE

From Page to Stage
Riding the Shakespeare Shuttle

In Part One of this study I used Levin's critique of suspicious reading and Taylor's theory of playgoing to illustrate a model of stage-centered criticism oriented toward the conditions of performance. My objection to the model is motivated by the belief that an approach that proscribes large chunks of interpretation simply because they are "readerly" and deemed unactable is per se not an adequate model. By this date there is enough competent and persuasive analysis of Shakespeare's language to make such an approach seem blinkered and theoretically suspect. Complex readings need not be judgmental, need not be cynical, need not be allegorical, need not be ironic, but even if they are, it is no argument against them to insist that the author of Shakespeare's plays couldn't have intended to elicit those readings; it is at best an arbitrary and, I suspect, a moral preference, not a theoretically based critique. My aim, however, is not simply to criticize the critique but to show that the theatrical model contains and suppresses the seeds of a different theoretical framework that will generate and validate alternative reading practices. I tried to expropriate that framework from Taylor's theory in the closing pages of Part One and to demonstrate it in Part Two.

The theatrical model does not by any means ignore the text, but it regulates scrutiny in accordance with the constraints and opportunities of performance. The literary model initially ignores this regulation and gives permission to readerly techniques that may produce effects that seem too minute or too complex to be digested in performance. It begins from the premise outlawed

139

by proponents of the theatrical model; its cardinal principle is a compendium of the cardinal sins Levin ascribes to the Age of the Reading. But it proceeds by a process of correction *toward* performance, or at least toward performability, taking account of theatrical circumstances but ignoring the constraints imposed by actual playgoing. Centered on the practice of imaginary audition, attentive to the structure and conditions of theater, maintaining the fiction of performance as a control on reading yet firmly committed to the practice of decelerated microanaylsis, the literary model of stage-centered reading perforce shuttles back and forth between two incompatible modes of interpretation, reading and playgoing. Whether one chooses to privilege the page or the stage, neither can do without the other. Any performance of a play actualizes what is (always) already an imagined performance, an imaginary performance, and this prior virtual status is inseparable from the interpretive reading that led to it.

Perhaps the most difficult and problematic feature of imaginary audition derives from its focus on what speech-act theorists call the performative and illocutionary dimension of language, a focus complicated by the attempt to analyze what may be called reflexive illocution. Before moving to the main body of my conclusion I want to comment on this complication by returning briefly to Porter's attempt, discussed above in Chapter 3, to approach *Richard II* through speech-act analysis. In that discussion I noted that Porter reduces *Richard II* to a play about speech-act theory. His reading dead-ends in the turnaround of the same circularity that Fish discovered in his own application of speech-act theory to Shakespeare: "*Coriolanus* is a speech-act play for me because it is with speech-act theory in mind that I approached the play in the first place." [1] But the high quality of Porter's insights carries them beyond the limits of the theory and solicits transplantation to a less localized interpretive field.

To take one example, Porter builds up the idea of "soliloquy-like" dialogue from the observation that in Richard's speech "direction of address" is characteristically unmarked and nonspecific and that throughout the play this produces "the subtle effect of his talking to himself even when he appears to be talking to others" (*Drama of Speech Acts,* 40–41). My debt to this insight is registered in some of the remarks I made in Part Two about the dimension of soliloquy in dialogue. But I also discussed the dialogical dimension within soliloquy and related it both to Richard's interlocutory encounters and to the interior motivational drama. Porter's application of speech-act theory follows the Austin/Searle paradigm in ignoring the possibility of analyzing *reflexive* illocutionary action, but the omission seems arbitrary, since the theory generates instruments for such an analysis. Furthermore, Porter's thesis discourages attention to the relations between reflexive and dialogical illocution. This leads to the standard line about Richard: "His tendency toward soliloquy manifests his tending toward solipsism and isolation." The next sentence leaps over dialogical illocution to Richard's penchant for theatrical self-representation: "Yet at the same time his unmarked direction of address manifests his completely public quality—the sense of him as sheer appearance, existing for, and only in the consciousness of, a general audience" (41). But if we take dialogical illocution into account—and 3.2 encourages us to do so, since (Porter notwithstanding) there are several instances of marked address directed at Aumerle and Scroope— the tendency toward soliloquy does not manifest solipsism so much as auditory voyeurism focused experimentally on the effects of self-representation.

Interrelating reflexive and dialogical illocution leads to further revisions that bring out the latent force of Porter's approach. Thus "Here, cousin, seize the crown" is by no means an idle "exercitive" but a classic instance of a "happy" speech act. In Austin's terminology, an exercitive "is a decision that something is to be so" and "it is advocacy that it should be so"; "it is an award" and "it is a sentence." Among his examples of exercitives the following characterize different aspects of the action specified by Richard's utterance to Bolingbroke: "command," "appoint," "bequeath," "resign," and "degrade." Among the typical contexts he lists, "Here, cousin, seize the crown" would seem to be an instance of "advice, exhortation, and petition," of "enablements, orders, sentences, and annulments," and of "filling offices and appointments, candidatures, elections, admissions, resignations, dismissals, and applications."[2] The wryness is partly Austin's own, a function of the self-deposing—or, as Fish calls it, the "self-consuming"—thrust of his project.[3] His categories, examples, and studiedly "rebarbative" terminology (Austin, *How to Do Things,* 151) are displayed with an air of dutiful embarrassment that dramatizes the project's unraveling, its unhappiness. If this wryness bleeds into Richard's project, it is because Shakespeare represents him as engaged in a similar unraveling the motive for which is touched on but not worked out in Porter's remarks on Richard's self-construction through inauthentic utterance.

I don't deny that Richard is, in a certain respect, self-absorbed and detached; my claim is only that the respect has little to do with solipsism or poetic sensibility but much to do with voyeurism and rhetoricopolitical awareness, and that the difference between these two views of Richard can be traced to divergent assumptions about the scope and structure of imaginary audition in the reading of drama. When Richard's speech is examined in abstraction from its interlocutory context—when it is read, we might say, solipsistically—the detachment becomes solipsistic. But when it is approached within that context via a synthesis of imaginary aural perspectives—listening with the ears of Carlisle or Scroope to Richard, listening with Richard's ears to their speech, to his speech, and to what he might imagine they do and don't hear in his words—solipsistic detachment becomes voyeuristic detachment.

In presenting this approach I have tried to give focus to a theory and practice of textual dramaturgy that feature complex acts of imaginary audition and to demonstrate the interpretive difference made by a particular kind of stage-centered reading. At the beginning of this study I mentioned the contrast postulated by proponents of the New Histrionicism between the Slit-eyed Analyst and the Wide-eyed Playgoer, personifications of bad and good reading, the former scornful of theatrical constraints and conditions, the latter respectful of them. I distinguished the psychological constraints on playgoing from the structured relations and circumstances of theater, and I proposed to chart a course between Analyst and Playgoer by ignoring the constraints and attending to the circumstances. But as my reading of 3.2 has shown, the literary model of stage-centered reading stipulates two constraints of another sort. First, plays are to be imagined not as poems, films, videotapes, or life slices but *as* plays, and as plays staged according to the conditions and conventions of the kind of theater that Shakespeare's plays represent. Second, those conditions and conventions are to provide guidelines for picking out relations within the drama that can be explicated or illuminated by the structure of playwright/actor/character/audience relationships. The first constraint is obviously a basic component of the approach demonstrated in the preceding analysis of 3.2, a constraint imposed in every moment of interpretive inquiry. The second constraint, less fundamental, may be brought to bear on interpretation whenever the language of the play suggests that dramatic relationships are conceived under the aspect of theatrical relationships. This includes not only overt metatheatrical passages in which theater is an *object* of representation but also all passages in which the structure of theatrical relationships may be seen to operate as an analogical *means* of representation, for example, in the conduct and effect of Richard's complex histrionic performance.

If I insist that the reading I have given is, in the respects just noted, stage-centered, it is equally important to insist that it remains a *reading*, that the conditions it observes are those not of unmediated performance but of the graphic inscription of texts. Perhaps the simplest and most obvious of these conditions is the possibility of deceleration. It is by slowing down the interlocutory drama, by holding it still in order to tease out its meanings, that I arrive at the picture of Richard engaged in the politics of the speech event. But deceleration, the armchair reader's privilege, is not enough. Slowing lines down deprives them of their force as speech acts. They must be reaccelerated so that we may imagine them flying by, and this is especially important for Richard's speeches. Only by imagining words spoken at normal tempo can we fully appreciate the peculiar power Shakespeare bestows on his protagonist—the rhetorical aggressiveness with which Richard floods his auditors with more meanings than the ear can catch, the joy with which he races through one overdetermined text after another. Reacceleration establishes the mimetic condition for detecting his auditory voyeurism; it allows us to imagine the inverse eavesdropping of a speaker whose speech "listens" to what his auditors do not hear and creates discrepant awarenesses by hoarding surplus meanings.

My emphasis on decelerated close reading exists in tension with an emphasis pitched more broadly at the level of what I have been calling the *motivational drama* and the *scenario,* a level that the solipsistic view of Richard notably ignores. Since the connotations of the two italicized terms are incompatible, I think I should explain why I have decided to use the second one even though it violates the scruple behind my choice of the first. For *motivational drama* is meant to denote what a character's language shows him to be moved by even when it doesn't provide the evidence for deciding whether he is aware or unaware of the motive, whether the actions and strings of action issuing forth from the motive appear to be intended or unintended, and whether discernible patterns of intention reinforce, ignore, or repress the motivational pattern. *Scenario,* however, and such related terms as *project* and *shadowplot* connote the kind of purpose, intention, and planning that active infinitives express: "to lose the crown, to get oneself deposed," and so on. This usage is misleading but I risk it because I want to center attention on the planlike character and constraining narrative logic of motivational patterns.

Scenario is also misleading in another way: it implies a preformulated plan, a pattern laid out at the beginning. Reading synchronically, we abstract the motivational pattern from the motivational drama. A synchronic view of the text, which is a privilege of any reading after the first one, is also a synoptic view. The patterns may be laid out in diagram form. But diachronic reading redirects attention to the limited frame of local dramaturgy and to the moment-by-moment elaboration of the pattern in speech events. *Elaboration* is not synonymous with *unfolding:* a scenario that is "worked out" by one or more characters need not be one that preexisted in infolded form. It is only from the synchronic standpoint, or from the standpoint of a character who deliberately plans a scenario and the practices by which it is actualized, that we can speak of the pattern "unfolding." The most obvious examples are those of such villainous scenarists as Edmund, Iago, and Richard III. There, the character's perspective and the reader's synchronic perspective overlap to a considerable degree.

The scenario of Richard II is not like this. Though I think it is discernible to the reader from the beginning, the degree to which Richard appears aware of it seems to me to be impossible to determine. Viewed synchronically, it may be said to "unfold" according to a logic that is consistently sustained throughout the play, and thus it has been too easy for me to discuss "Richard's scenario" as if he intentionally controlled its development. I am not ruling out the possibility that an interpretive case may be made for this hypothesis. I am only saying that the evidence I have been able to assemble can't either confirm or disconfirm the hypothesis. I have explored a framework of complex audition that involves the reification of an auditor or observer within, and in terms of this framework I have deduced from the language a hypothetical activity of auditory voyeurism. But I can say no more than that I *imagine* this observer to watch the scenario unfold.

I am aware that this formulation begs questions in the same way that Sartre's *mauvaise foi*, or the Freudian notion of censor Sartre was criticizing, begs questions. Nevertheless, it is important to allow for this fuzziness and inadequacy if for no other reason than to keep before us the inapplicability to fictional speakers of concepts devised for the analysis of actual persons. It is important, that is, to maintain considerable flexibility in the deployment of such concepts as character and consciousness. In fact I would go so far as to opt for a consistent inconsistency, to premise that we can sometimes determine what a speaker intends to say and sometimes not, and that decisions about this may vary from moment to moment as well as from interpreter to interpreter. The possibility of deciding whether any passage is ironic or not and whether, if it is ironic, it is an instance of intentional or structural irony presupposes this determination. For if we can't decide what a speaker means to say, then we can't argue that he means one thing and says another or that he unintentionally says one thing while meaning another. At least we can't do this in any simple and direct manner.

Suppose, for example, that there is general agreement that in the phrase "Uneasy lies the head that wears the crown," "lies" is a pun. This line concludes the soliloquy on insomnia in which Henry IV self-pityingly compares the effect of the responsibilities of state on the king to the easier lot of his "happy low" subjects. The alternate meaning of "lies," which suggests that the "head" lies uneasily, shifts the meaning of the line from a thematic summary of the soliloquy to a reflexive comment on the kind of speech act it is: the king is lying, has been lying, to himself in blaming his malaise on cares of state, and the context—previous information and the remainder of this scene—suggests a different cause, that is, "uneasy lies the head that *stole* the crown."[4] We can agree that both the statement and its context encourage this reading without having to agree on the speaker's relation to it. Is Henry aware or unaware of the pun? Is the utterance mordant and self-lacerating, is the pun something he suddenly stumbles on and recognizes, or is he unaware that his language is giving him away? My decision to read "lies" ambiguously is strictly a semiotic decision, a matter of linguistic interpretation that precedes and is unaffected by any psychological disposition I may subsequently make of it. Meanings or messages may be excavated from the language before the excavator decides whether they are meant or unmeant, heard or unheard, by speakers and auditors and before he decides what kind of psychological framework he will use to condition the development and dramatic articulation of the meanings. I can provisionally place speakers and hearers in brackets and act as if the text is directly communicating its messages to me. Having appropriated—or "received"—the messages, I may then decide how to dispose of them.

This procedure implies a three-level interpretive hierarchy. The most fundamental—and also the most antitheatrical—level of analysis construes the play synchronically and diachronically as a continuous text ("text" in the "writerly" sense of that word), and it is at this level that we find most of the evidence for what I have been describing as motivational dramas and scenarios. At the second level is the analysis of the text as *script,* by which I mean the dialogical "sides" of fictive speech acts and events, and since I believe that Shakespearean politics is most highly concentrated in and as the interlocutory power plays that comprise the script, I look more to that level than to abstract institutional analysis for insights into the politics of any fictive community. At the third level, text and script are interrogated for profiles of the speakers they constitute. Of course I don't offer this scheme as a set of operating instructions. No one should try to do interpretation by the numbers, moving obediently from one level to the next. The scheme serves mainly to distinguish and interrelate different kinds of interpretive operations. It does, however, give logical priority to the first level in order to safeguard the generativity but also the indeterminacy and incompleteness of the text. And it has another purpose, which is to promote the hypothesis that a character or dramatic person is the effect rather than the cause of his or her speech and of our interpretation.

Indeed, there is no reason why we should defer to the authority of speakers and their proprietary rights over language any more than we do to those of the author. But just as we used to quarry the text for information about the author and his context, so we can now shift our focus and quarry it for information about the speakers and their dramatic community. We can explore the complexity and ambivalence of Henry's language "objectively," that is, apart from Henry, and we can then ask what it tells us about Henry—what range of assertions we're entitled to make about the states of mind, the intentions and motives, the fears and desires, the awareness and unawareness of the speaker to whose name the language is formally assigned. For if the language exists "before" and "outside of" any character or consciousness we construct on the basis of the evidence we find in it, then, during interpretation, the language comes to "speak" the character and to speak *about* him. In no way is it an immediate expression of his "interiority." Rather, it offers suggestions and directions for a portrait or a set of portraits that readers, actors, and directors proceed to draw. From this standpoint speech is not the property of the speaker; the speaker is the property of the language. The language may be "psychoanalyzed" apart from the speaker, and readers may agree in their analysis—may agree, for example, on the presence of a specific set of effects, motives, or "moves" in a stretch of language—but still disagree when it comes to deciding what that analysis tells them about the speaker.

To return to Richard: if, in "listening" to his speech, I sense the presence of an auditor within the speaker, I am not compelled to take a stand on the question of the speaker's awareness of that auditor. That presence is inferred from Richard's language when his interlocutory behavior is interpreted within the framework of imaginary audition. Though the framework entails diachronic analysis, it subjects it to pronounced deceleration, as I noted above, and it is only under those conditions that the inferred activity can be explored. Stage-centered reading has also to allow for the imagined reacceleration of speech to the tempo of performance and has to adjust its hypotheses accordingly. When I slow down the tempo, the auditor within Richard and his interaction with Richard's scenario come into imaginary focus. Deceleration materializes the auditory voyeur secretly attentive to the progress of his ars moriendi, cherishing his audience's ignorance of it, teasing them with glimpses of it, rehearsing for his confrontation with Bolingbroke, working on his autothanatography.

Decelerated microanalysis thus enlarges and emblematically fixes features not discernible in the normal rhythm of communication. But when I reaccelerate the tempo to imagine the mimesis of normal speech, the quasi-allegorical figure of the scenarist tends to dissolve in the rapid flow of interlocutory exchange, where its scattered traces are picked up in the passing play of lexical, rhetorical, and tonal effects, effects produced by a speaker who shares neither my synchronic perspective nor my privilege of reading. In the imaginary audition of normal tempo "the production of effects" stands out as the primary effect at which his performance aims: Richard's speech represents a speaker intent on representing himself by displaying wildly inconsistent reactions to bad news and by converting communicative exchanges into challenges to—as well as opportunities for—continued performative domination. But this impression tallies with the standard view of the Player King—wordy, self-dramatizing and -indulgent, scene-hogging, unpredictable, self-destructive, politically inept—and could have been gathered by the Wide-eyed Playgoer without all the complicated business of deceleration and reacceleration. It is also the view reflected by the uneasy responses of Richard's onstage audience in 3.2 and in later scenes. Yet there is a radical difference between their innocent version of this view and the one obtained by first decelerating the text: theirs occludes the sustained political thrust behind the pattern of self-undoing and the drama of despair, occludes also the scenario (already forming in 3.2) aimed at using the crown as a mousetrap to catch and wound the conscience of the next king. Thus one result of reaccelerating the text and imagining the normal tempo of interlocutory speech is to increase the reader's appreciation of the discrepant awareness produced by Richard's auditory voyeurism. We sense how much is withheld from an audience that can only hear and see, how much is occulted in the text they cannot read.

What, then, of an offstage audience that shares this limited view of Richard, an audience made up of the Wide-eyed Playgoer and all readers who aspire to that musical condition? Does this innocent audience in effect create itself in the image of the onstage audience? Does it receive Richard's speech in the same manner—undecelerated, unreaccelerated? Does it, to invert Desdemona's haunting phrase, understand his words but not their fury? Or, not quite understanding why he says what he says the way he says it, does the innocent audience hear the burnished fury in his words and stir in perplexed uneasiness? Does impatience rustle through it, or embarrassment, or, perhaps, the faint suspicion that it is being mocked? And, finally, to put the question toward which these questions lead, does the relation of *Richard II* to its offstage audience in the theater mirror that of Richard II to his onstage audience in the drama?

It is no doubt perverse to find that the desire of theater burning through Shakespeare's texts is crossed by a certain despair of theater, of the theater that seduces them and the theater they seduce; a despair inscribed in the auditory voyeurism with which the spoken language outruns its auditors, dropping golden apples along the way to divert the greedy ear that longs to devour its discourse. Yet this is the inference gleaned from a practice of reading that shuttles back and forth between two incompatible modifications of performance tempo, deceleration and reacceleration. I don't think we need to repeat the obvious historical reasons, specific to the forms the institutions of literacy have been taking in our century and society, why the Shakespeare shuttle can no longer be a one-way ride from page to stage. But need we resign ourselves to the anachronism denoted by "no longer"? How can we be sure that the author of Shakespeare's texts wanted them always to end their journey at the theater, to be fully consumed and digested in performance? I shall devote my concluding discussion to another story, an alternative hypothesis about the historical context that could have given rise to the diffidence, the ambivalence, of an unending interpretive shuttle.

I suggested at the beginning of this study that although Taylor's theoretical ideal of the Wide-eyed Playgoer is hypothetical and hyperbolic in an age of mass literacy and education, it may have been less so in Shakespeare's time, and therefore that Shakespeare might well have been cognizant of writing in a situation that necessarily produced a relationship of discrepant awarenesses between author and audience. Theater-centered critics would argue that Shakespeare's success lies in overcoming the discrepancy and bringing the audience at least partway up to his level. They would surely agree with Terence Hawkes that "Man," as he once quaintly put it, "is the Talking Animal," and Shakespeare wrote *for* that Animal:

> Shakespeare's plays seem to embody the notion that the essence of human nature lies in the efficacy of oral, face to face communication. Man is the Talking Animal, and Shakespeare's plays were written for an audience of talkers who communicated primarily in that mode, since its alternative—that of reading and writing— had yet to become dominant. Drama, not then considered part of "literature," itself becomes in these plays a recurrent symbol of communication at its most efficacious. Fully to trust Shakespeare is fully to trust his firm faith in the capacities of man's talking nature, and in the play as the communicative medium which best exemplifies and embodies that.[5]

One might equally well imagine, however, that Shakespeare's firm faith was shaken by the fact that he, unlike Man, was a Writing Animal, and that—in common with many other members of his species—he writes about and against as well as for the Talking Animal, especially since this Animal not only talks but smokes, eats, hisses, pisses, panders, whores, and in other ways impedes efficacious performance of the Bard's attempts at face-to-face communication.

Unlike Taylor and other proponents of the New Histrionicism, Hawkes thinks "live" Shakespeare is now dead in theater because theater has become Theater, a high-culture ritual that testifies to the hegemony of literacy and Literature in bourgeois society. He suggests that the best way to revive Shakespeare's Talking Animals, and Shakespeare *as* a Talking Animal, may be to shift from the sacred precincts of the text-ridden theater to the "live" secular electricity of television (123–24). Hawkes is right if he thinks this is a good way to kill the Writing Animal, but since television bears the marks of the literate and postliterate claws of corporate interests, and since the living room is the stage for bourgeois rituals at whatever level (high, middlebrow, mass), his logic leaves something to be desired. The Elizabethan public theater has less resemblance to a living room than to a carnival. This analogy has often been drawn, perhaps most recently by Michael Bristol, who argues that carnival and Elizabethan drama share "a more or less coherent series of images and formal devices" of travesty and clownish misrule, the instruments by which plebeian culture laughs both at itself and at official culture.[6] More important, theater "shares with Carnival the experience of a liminal time outside the schedules of honest work and honest devotion; in fact this is one basis for the polemic against the stage and for the frequently asserted charge that the theater is a resort of idleness. The time of performance is a festive time in which symbolic activity or play replaces productive labor" (647).

The carnivalesque themes of the drama, however, were not contained within the parentheses of performance. As M. C. Bradbrook explains, they spilled out into the surrounding actualities of social conflict:

> Players aspired to the condition of merchants and citizens; to attain it, they masqueraded as members of the gentlemanly profession of serving men. . . . It was the men to whose condition they aspired who provided the strongest opposition. The merchants were their steadiest opponents. . . . The City merchants whose . . . fine new houses so prominently displayed their own superfluous wealth, themselves did not always observe traditional formulations, but this only sharpened their disapproval of upstarts like the common players.
>
> The Elizabethan opposition made the double charge that plays taught bawdry, trickery and baseness; and that the audience did not attend to the plays, but were engaged in bawdry, trickery and baseness of their own.[7]

Beyond that, the plays dramatized the contradictions in the regnant discourses of the playgoers' culture: gender, generation, hierarchy, moral ideology, and religion. Bradbrook's brilliant comment on revenge tragedy suggests how deeply this mimesis could penetrate into major sources of anxiety affecting players and playgoers alike:

> This "black tragedy" embodied in figures, drawn from the enemy realms of Spain and papal Italy, the perpetual tragic issues of guilt and sacrifice; it allowed the projection of deep fears, the exorcism of guilt which actors and audiences shared. In the terrifying figures of Hieronimo the Revenger as created by Edward Alleyn, *the punitive and denunciatory aspects of the religious attack on the stage were unconsciously absorbed and mastered.* Within the tragedies of the public stage may be seen, contained and assimilated, the rage and fear which the actor aroused and the mirror image of that rage and fear evoked in himself.   (130)

In all these respects, the theater process involves a double mode of representation: it constructs the audience metonymically as a representative standing for the "world" traversed by the discourses the drama imitates (= represents). The audience's culture, its desires, its illusions and defenses, its motivational patterns are written into the drama, displaced in the slant reflections provided by the literary and cultural discourses that circulate through the fictive community. Representation *in the presence of* an audience is thus at the same time representation *of* that audience. The audience has in that sense been fictionalized, its actual presence effaced and supplanted by a representation, the first world extended from and crystallized around the second through the medium of the theater process that initially distinguishes and ultimately identifies them. What Elizabethan subjects get away from when they go to the theater in order to play audience confronts them in the play: the strains or contradictions in the cultural discourses that make them subjects. If they disregard or refuse that confrontation they are even more fully inscribed in a drama that thematizes such disregard or refusal. When, in addition, the dramatic fiction recursively displays its putatively extratheatrical events in terms of the theater process—when dramatic persons speak as if aware of playing roles, performing before audiences, putting on plays, and so forth in the second world—then the theatricality reflected into the first world the audience stands for tends to fictionalize that world's "realities." The representation of the theater process within dramatic fiction frees it from the contingency and evanescence of actual stage performance; theater, play, actors, dramatic persons, and audience are occulted by the drama and sedimented into its text.

Bradbrook's comments on the prominent entertainment function of public theater suggest another reason why the Shakespearean critique of theater would target the limits of the system of innocent playgoing: "Drama was mixed up in the public mind with the athletics of fencing, with bear-baiting, dancing on the ropes and other activities." Since sermons were among the "many forms of entertainment" plays competed with, the simplest auditors "would have been trained . . . to be edified by much they imperfectly understood," yet

> in an open air, daylight theater, attention must be less exclusively given to the stage, and more to the complete concourse. At an inn, there must also have been some coming and going throughout the performance. . . . Whether at inn or theater, the audience's mood would naturally be one of pastime; they had no duty to attend to the performers, being involved in the give and take which was part of the show, slipping out for refreshment or dodging the shower of fireworks. (96, 98–99)

Whether or not the audiences at public theaters were dominated by "privileged playgoers," as Ann Jennalie Cook claims, is less important than the character of the theater process in which they participated. Cook tries to defend the proposition that the greatness of Elizabethan drama owed much to the challenge offered playwrights by the superior education and sophistication of a constituency that could afford a relatively expensive pastime.[8] Yet in marshalling evidence of the playgoers' prosperity (97–215) she only endorses the picture Bradbrook gives of diversions that would greatly diminish the challenge: food, drink, tobacco; "cutpurses, courtesans, and cozeners" who "did not patronize the theater because they felt an overwhelming desire to see the plays but . . . because they found profit among the other playgoers. The presence of such social parasites pointed toward an audience with plenty of money to be stolen or to be squandered on pleasure" (241). It also pointed toward negotiations that would distract attention from the stage "to the complete concourse."

This may be why Richard Levin once asserted that most of the plays were commissioned for court performance.[9] The assertion is consistent with the premises of the argument he later developed: it defends against the disquieting idea that the responses of audiences such as those described by Bradbrook should set the standards and limits for the subsequent interpretive consensus he established as a norm and ascribes to all audiences from Shakespeare's time up to the catastrophic consequences of New Criticism and the Age of the Reading. But Levin's audience originated in the public as well as the private theater. The standards he would have us follow were thus in part set by a theater the visual appeal of whose spectacles "was surely directed toward satisfying middle-class aspirations. The costumes . . . were real court clothes, and their splendor, in a society whose sumptuary laws regulated even styles of dress, would have given a merchant or tradesman the richest sense he was ever likely to have of how the aristocratic life looked in action."[10] Even if for our interpretive cynosure we look to the audience at court rather than the one in the public theater, we find that this version of the theater process has its own distractions:

> In the world of the court . . . theatricals were, like the other events that took place in the Hall and the Banqueting House, cele-

brations of royal power and assertions of aristocratic community. . . . Dramas at court were not entertainments in the simple and dismissive sense we usually apply to the term. They were expressions of the age's most profound assumptions about the monarchy. They included strong elements of ritual and communion, often explicitly religious; and to participate in such a production involved far more than simply watching a play. . . . At these performances what the rest of the spectators watched was not a play but the queen at a play, and their response would have been not simply to the drama, but to the relationship between the drama and its primary audience, the royal spectator. (7–9)

If these are two audiences Shakespeare wrote for, they surely are not the only two, since he wrote about them as well as for them. His texts direct response "not simply to the drama, but to the relationship between the drama and its primary audience," the Elizabethan subjects, royal and otherwise, who are constructed by and interact with the cultural discourses speaking through them. To borrow Fish's terms, for his primary audiences and their avatars Shakespeare wrote self-satisfying artifacts which, viewed awry, become self-consuming representations of the self-satisfying experience. Shakespearean theater was, like drama, an object of representation, a fiction. He taught us how to imagine playgoing. That is, his texts teach us that playgoing is an imaginary activity, an institutional fiction, and that when we go to the theater and actualize the fiction our engagement with the roles, conventions, and interests of playgoing is still, in that respect, imaginary. Having committed his texts to the particular constraints of the forms of theater described by Bradbrook and Orgel, he transcends—or perhaps we could say he deconstructs—the theater process by decomposing its elements and distributing them throughout the texture of the drama's second world. The theatrical, metatheatrical, and antitheatrical aspects of the text preserve an image of the process that implies a certain kind of virtual playgoer, one who conforms to the conventions and conditions depicted above. Barry Weller remarks of Shakespeare's characters that they "frequently manifest the desire to be recognized as something other than they 'seem', that is, to belie the visible and audible evidence of their presence onstage by suggesting that it does not and cannot adequately represent what they are."[11] I submit that the plays manifest the same desire.

Stephen Greenblatt has argued that although a play such as *Henry V* is deeply subversive, the doubts Shakespeare raises about Henry's bad faith "serve not to rob the king of his charisma but to heighten it, precisely as they heighten the theatrical interest of the play." Confronted by the "gap between real and ideal . . . the spectators are induced to make up the difference, to invest in the illusion of magnificence," to produce "a celebration, a collective panegyric to . . . the charismatic leader." From the play's politics of audience co-optation he extracts the general message that "all kings are 'decked' out by the imaginary forces of the spectators, and a sense of the limitations of king or theater only excites a more compelling exercise of those forces." Therefore "it is not at all clear that *Henry V* can be successfully performed as subversive."[12] Performance contains the subversiveness. But isn't that containment a theme of the text that represents the virtual theater and performance? Greenblatt's account in fact suggests a carnivalesque variation on Bristol's observation that theater "shares with Carnival the experience of a liminal time outside the schedules of honest work and honest devotion": outside, behind, beneath, within the "schedules of honest" performance and entertainment is the continuous carnival of the text.

Notes

PROLOGUE

1. Sigurd Burckhardt, *Shakespearean Meanings* (Princeton: Princeton University Press, 1967), vii–viii.

2. J. L. Styan, *The Shakespeare Revolution* (1977; rpt. Cambridge: Cambridge University Press, 1983); Richard Levin, *New Readings vs. Old Plays: Recent Trends in the Reinterpretation of English Renaissance Drama* (Chicago: University of Chicago Press, 1979); Gary Taylor, *Moment by Moment by Shakespeare* (London: Macmillan, 1985).

3. Harry Berger, Jr., "Text against Performance in Shakespeare: The Example of *Macbeth*," in *The Power of Forms in the English Renaissance*, ed. Stephen Greenblatt (Norman, Okla.: Pilgrim Books, 1982), 49–81. See the critical response by Richard Levin in "The New Refutation of Shakespeare," *Modern Philology* 83 (1985): 123–41. See also the sensible criticism by Barbara Hodgdon in "Parallel Practices, or the *Un*-Necessary Difference," *Kenyon Review* N.S. 7 (Summer 1985): 57–65. As Levin and others have made me see, my argument about the constraints of performance was sadly one-sided (more so than I intended). Because my perspective was strictly textual I had nothing to say about the advantages of performance or about the constraints of reading relative to audition. This detracted from the point I was trying to make, which was that Shakespeare's texts often *represent* the constraints of performance in a variety of ways.

4. The represented constraints are also psychological, and in subsequent essays (see next two notes) I characterized them in terms of what I have called the Lafew principle after the old courtier in *All's Well That Ends Well*, from whom its text is borrowed: "we make trifles of terrors, ensconcing ourselves into seeming knowledge when we should submit ourselves to an unknown fear" (2.3.3–6).

5. Harry Berger, Jr., "Sneak's Noise: Rumor and Detextualization in *2 Henry IV*," *Kenyon Review* N.S. 6 (Fall 1984): 58–78.

6. See my "Textual Dramaturgy: Representing the Limits of Theater in *Richard II*," *Theatre Journal* 39 (1987): 135–55, and "*Ars Moriendi* in Progress, or, John of Gaunt and the Practice of Strategic Dying," *Yale Journal of Criticism* 1 (1987): 39–65.

7. Walter Ong, "The Writer's Audience Is Always a Fiction," in his *Interfaces of the Word: Studies in the Evolution of Consciousness and Culture* (Ithaca: Cornell University Press, 1977), 53–81.

8. For critiques of this problem, see the following: John Frow, *Marxism and Literary History* (Cambridge: Harvard University Press, 1986), 182–87; Jonathan Culler, *On Deconstruction: Theory and Criticism after Structuralism* (Ithaca: Cornell University Press, 1982), 34–82; Christine Brooke-Rose, "The Readerhood of Man," in *The Reader in the Text: Essays on Audience and Interpretation,* ed. Susan Suleiman and Inge Crosman (Princeton: Princeton University Press, 1980), 120–48. Jane P. Tompkins's introductory and concluding essays in her anthology *Reader-Response Criticism: From Formalism to Post-Structuralism* (Baltimore: Johns Hopkins University Press, 1980) provide excellent analytical and historical contexts for an understanding of the problem.

PART ONE: INTRODUCTION

1. Styan, *The Shakespeare Revolution,* 237, 233, 235, 6, 169. On Bradbrook, Knight, and other academic critics see especially 160–79.

2. Harriett Hawkins, *The Devil's Party: Critical Counter-Interpretations of Shakespearian Drama* (Oxford: Clarendon Press, 1985), 61.

3. Philip McGuire, *Speechless Dialect: Shakespeare's Open Silences* (Berkeley and Los Angeles: University of California Press, 1985).

4. Norman Rabkin's *Shakespeare and the Common Understanding* (New York: The Free Press, 1967) and Burckhardt's *Shakespearean Meanings* were published in the same year (1967) and both coincidentally put the idea of complementarity into play.

5. Thus McGuire asserts that the three "themata" of classical physics—simplicity, completeness, causality—are also those that govern the textual paradigm. This is arguably not true of a great deal of "textual" interpretation. The analogy produces a straw man.

6. Taylor, *Moment by Moment,* vii.

7. Harriett Hawkins, "Critical Studies," in *Shakespeare Survey* 33 (1980): 183–84.

8. Since, as I indicated before, I have personally profited from being one of Levin's targets, the following critique should be taken in the spirit of sour grapes in which it was written. Levin's objections in "The New Refutation of Shakespeare" to my stumbling attempts to articulate the text-vs.-performance thesis are well taken and were helpful to me. I still feel myself stumbling in the present study, but thanks to Levin the issues have become clearer and I now see what's wrong with his approach as well as mine.

For a different critique of Levin, see Norman Rabkin, *Shakespeare and the Problem of Meaning* (Chicago: University of Chicago Press, 1981), 1–8, 22, 26–27.

More recently, Levin has isolated an extremist school of performance criticism to complement his varieties of slit-eyed analysis—critics who sometimes assert that the plays of Shakespeare and his contemporaries "can be really understood only in performance, or even that they really exist only in performance" ("Performance-Critics *vs.* Close Readers in the Study of English Renaissance Drama," *Modern Language Review* 81 [1986]: 547). On the basis of the evidence he assembles he finds that the claims of both factions "have no historical foundation" (559). Against performance-critics he argues that most of the Renaissance dramatists and many of their contemporaries "believed that plays existed, first and foremost, in the written texts," and against slit-eyed analysts he argues that "they also believed that these texts were written with a performance in mind, and therefore should be read as if they were being performed" (558). It gives me pleasure to note that on page 554 Levin quotes passages by Chapman, Ford, and others that entertain rough approximations to the process I am calling imaginary audition.

Although Levin's argument doesn't affect my claim that in Shakespeare's time the scope of literacy was more limited and that not many members of the audience in public theaters could have been expected to have read the plays they saw, it does provide evidence for my claim that playwrights may have written *about* and *against* their audiences as well as *for* them. Had I space for a fuller discussion of Levin's essay, I would take issue with the concept of "historical foundation" implicit in the kind of evidence he assembles.

CHAPTER ONE

1. When I write about the "text" of the play and describe it as if it had its own "intentions," I am doing the same thing; the only difference is that I am trying to avoid the appearance of committing what would nowadays be called the Author-function Fallacy.

2. Levin tries to clarify his notion of consensus in "Hazlitt on *Henry V*, and the Appropriation of Shakespeare," *Shakespeare Quarterly* 35 (1984): 137.

3. Stanley Wells, "Shakespeare Criticism since Bradley," in *A New Companion to Shakespeare Studies,* ed. Kenneth Muir and S. Schoenbaum (Cambridge: Cambridge University Press, 1971), 249. This and the preceding essay by M. A. Shaaber, "Shakespeare Criticism: Dryden to Bradley" (239–48), provide excellent overviews of critical change, concise yet detailed.

4. Shaaber, "Shakespeare Criticism," 246.

5. Gerald Eades Bentley, *The Profession of Dramatist in Shakespeare's Time* (Princeton: Princeton University Press, 1971), 108, 87, 55–56, 62, 8.

6. Andrew Gurr, *The Shakespearean Stage, 1574–1642* (Cambridge: Cambridge University Press, 1970), 149–50.

7. Jonas Barish, *The Antitheatrical Prejudice* (Berkeley and Los Angeles: University of California Press, 1981), 133.

8. Alvin Kernan, *The Playwright as Magician: Shakespeare's Image of the Poet in the English Public Theater* (New Haven: Yale University Press, 1979), 158.

9. Alvin Kernan, "Shakespeare's Stage Audiences: The Playwright's Reflections and Control of Audience Response," in *Shakespeare's Craft: Eight Lectures,* ed. Philip H. Highfill, Jr. (Carbondale: Southern Illinois University Press, 1982), 153–55.

10. See Taylor's shrewd speculations about the way audience expectations presented Shakespeare with a challenge in *Julius Caesar* and *Antony and Cleopatra* (*Moment by Moment,* 43–44); the whole discussion of the textual crux at *Julius Caesar* 3.1.47 is well worth reading (40–47).

11. Annabel Patterson, *Censorship and Interpretation: The Conditions of Writing and Reading in Early Modern England* (Madison: University of Wisconsin Press, 1984), 7.

12. Leo Strauss, *Persecution and the Art of Writing* (Westport, Conn.: Greenwood Press, 1952).

13. Gary Taylor, "Monopolies, Show Trials, Disaster, and Invasion: *King Lear* and Censorship," in *The Division of the Kingdoms,* ed. Taylor and Michael Warren (Oxford: Clarendon Press, 1984), 75–117.

14. Bentley, *The Profession of Dramatist,* 150–51.

15. Joel Hurstfield, *Freedom, Corruption and Government in Elizabethan England* (London: Jonathan Cape, 1973), 45.

16. Ernst Kantorowicz, *The King's Two Bodies: A Study in Medieval Political Theology* (Princeton: Princeton University Press, 1957), 20.

CHAPTER TWO

1. Taylor, *Moment by Moment,* 166–67. I cite this passage only for its usefulness as a symptom of Taylor's theoretical commitments, not for its intrinsic force or interest. As a characterization of the practical alternatives open to the interpreter who ignores "the chronological imperative of performance," this and the paragraph that follows strike me as sheer nonsense.

2. Taylor's concept of innocence is a little broad-planed, or fuzzy. We should distinguish, as he doesn't, between dramatic and theatrical succession or "temporality." The former is the property of fiction, the before-and-after of the narrative line, while the latter is the property of

the particular theatrical occasion on which the drama is performed. For a playgoer who knows a play there may yet be novelty in the details of each performance—in the interaction of the players with each other, the audience, and the characters they stage. So there are different kinds and degrees of innocence. The experienced reader may be innocent or ignorant of theater, and vice versa. He or she may be innocent of Shakespeare's plays, of one play, of a particular production of that play; or innocent of critical (especially New Critical) studies of the play; or innocent of Taylor's book.

3. For a list of those resources, see the summary he gives on p. 48 of "the themes and techniques of my own aesthetic."

4. This idea was anticipated by A. R. Humphreys in the concluding paragraph of his introduction to *Henry V* in the New Penguin Shakespeare (Harmondsworth: Penguin, 1968), 49. Humphreys argues that *Henry V* requires one to be "willingly naive rather than innocent" and to "give one's scepticism a day off and let one's gusto serve instead." Taylor's view of *Henry V* in *Moment by Moment* and even more emphatically in the introduction to his recent edition of the play for the Oxford Shakespeare series is that the play is patterned first to arouse our skepticism and suspicion and then to overcome it by soliciting our enthusiastic support for Henry's behavior and his cause. For an ideologically more sophisticated treatment of this pattern, and one that leaves me with the feeling that Humphreys and Taylor have been co-opted, see Stephen Greenblatt, "Invisible Bullets: Renaissance Authority and Its Subversion, *Henry IV* and *Henry V*," in *Political Shakespeare: New Essays in Cultural Materialism*, ed. Jonathan Dollimore and Alan Sinfield (Ithaca: Cornell University Press, 1985), 18–47, esp. 41–45.

5. Taylor, *Moment by Moment*, 39 and 242n. 17, which paraphrase and refer to the following sentence from Stanley Fish's *Self-Consuming Artifacts* (Berkeley and Los Angeles: University of California Press, 1972): "The objectivity of the text is an illusion, and moreover a dangerous illusion, because it is so physically convincing" (400). The critique of the New Critical emphasis on "objectivity" and "spatialism" is a major feature of the strategy by which Fish tries to distinguish his own kinetic and linear or moment-by-moment fiction of reading from that of his literary "fathers." That critique is inaccurate because much New Critical practice focused "kinetically" on the "experience" of the fictive speaker or persona, and Fish's practice is less different than he claims because he often models the experience of the reader on that of the speaker. Confused treatments of the concepts of linearity and sequence and of the status of the reader (virtual or empirical?) beset Fish's theory, practice, and descriptions of method and are evaded rather than clarified in his later move to the concept of interpretive communities. Those confusions are also apparent in Taylor's audience-response theory and practice. They crop up, for example, in two statements in the same pas-

sage (39): first, that language is "by nature sequential," and, second, that the text is sequential. Given the amount of attention that has been devoted to the difference between the sequentiality of oral language and that of written language, those statements are surprisingly obtuse.

6. Culler, *On Deconstruction,* 100–101.

7. Barbara Johnson, "Mallarmé and Austin," in her *The Critical Difference: Essays in the Contemporary Rhetoric of Reading* (Baltimore: Johns Hopkins University Press, 1980), 60. Emile Benveniste makes the same point in *Problems in General Linguistics,* trans. Mary Elizabeth Meek (Coral Gables: University of Miami Press, 1971), 236. The Derrida-Johnson critique of Austin was placed in question by Stanley Fish, who, in "With the Compliments of the Author: Reflections on Austin and Derrida" (*Critical Inquiry* 8 [1982]: 693–721), reads *How to Do Things with Words* as a self-consuming text and shows how it anticipates the deconstructive problematic; and by Shoshana Felman in her brilliant *The Literary Speech Act: Don Juan with J. L. Austin, or, Seduction in Two Languages,* trans. Catherine Porter (Ithaca: Cornell University Press, 1983).

8. Fish, "With the Compliments of the Author," 704.

9. Jacques Derrida, "Signature Event Context," in his *Margins of Philosophy,* trans. Alan Bass (Chicago: University of Chicago Press, 1982), 311.

PART TWO: INTRODUCTION

1. This paragraph partly echoes and partly departs from my "*Ars Moriendi* in Progress," 50.

CHAPTER THREE

1. Leonard Barkan, "The Theatrical Consistency of *Richard II,*" *Shakespeare Quarterly* 29 (1978): 15–16.

2. James Winny, *The Player King: A Theme of Shakespeare's Histories* (London: Chatto and Windus, 1968), 62. Compare the gardener's trope in the previous scene: "In your lord's scale is nothing but himself, / And some few vanities that make him light," while "all the English peers" are in Bolingbroke's balance, "And with that odds he weighs King Richard down" (3.4.84–89). That Richard's simile echoes this figure supports Winny's reading. The echo has been noted by Ernest B. Gilman in *The Curious Perspective: Literary and Pictorial Wit in the Seventeenth Century* (New Haven: Yale University Press, 1978), 121.

3. Peter Ure's gloss in the Arden edition, 136.

4. Barkan, "Theatrical Consistency," 16.

5. "While Bolingbroke is executing villainous Plantagenet allies,

Richard is making his own deposition inevitable by yielding to all demands before his rival can even make them" (Barkan, "Theatrical Consistency," 10). In some respects my emphasis on Richard's *political* efficacy was anticipated by Herbert R. Coursen in *The Leasing Out of England: Shakespeare's Second Henriad* (Washington: University Presses of America, 1982), 15–76. But Coursen and I practice very different styles of reading and reach different conclusions. He treats the play's sacramentalism as a transcendent reality behind (and informing) the language, a reality destroyed by Richard's kingship and Bolingbroke's usurpation. I treat sacramentalism as a language effect whose reality for the characters is continuously reproduced and manifested in the rhetorical indices to guilty conscience, to fear or desire of damnation and punishment, and to fear or desire of forgiveness.

6. Winny, *The Player King*, 58. The theme of self-destruction has often been noted but has been variously treated. See, for example, Wilbur Sanders, *The Dramatist and the Received Idea* (Cambridge: Cambridge University Press, 1968), 158–93, and John Blanpied, *Time and the Artist in Shakespeare's English Histories* (Newark: University of Delaware Press, 1983), 122–24.

7. For still another reading, see the excellent remarks of David Sundelson in *Shakespeare's Restorations of the Father* (New Brunswick: Rutgers University Press, 1983), 27–39. Sundelson also appreciates Winny's contribution but finds his analysis "vague" and tries to make it more precise by exploring the "regressive ladder" down which Richard moves from father to "competing brother" to "only son" to "mother's protected infant" (31). His thesis that "Richard will be first in misery, if not in might" and that he alternates like an infant between fantasies of omnipotence and of "delicious weakness" (35) is adroitly managed. My objection to this account is that Sundelson's allegiance to the explanatory schemes and myths of psychoanalysis leads him to interpret Richard's fantasies as psychological rather than rhetorical entities. He ignores the possibility that Richard *represents* those fantasies and that his motive for displaying them may or may not be grounded in the desires they embody.

8. Burckhardt argues that Richard "cannot reconcile his concept of kingship with the necessity of defending his title. . . . If the title is true, *God* will defend it. . . . If God will not defend it, it isn't true" (*Shakespearean Meanings*, 169–70). But in his concern over the succession theme Burckhardt swerves from the issue Richard is raising: if the king's title is true, will God defend his right to it even when he despoils his country? Is God "true"?

9. My tendency here and elsewhere is to defend against the flourishing industry of character judgment—against critics who spend time worrying whether characters are good or bad, whether they meet the critic's own high moral standards or fall short of them—on the grounds

that what a character thinks of himself, how he judges himself, is more interesting than what I think of him or how I judge him. See William L. Godshalk, *Patterning in Shakespearean Drama* (The Hague: Mouton, 1973), 85-86, and Godshalk's brief bibliography of judgmental criticism in n. 19.

10. Kantorowicz, *The King's Two Bodies*, 38, 27.

11. Richard Wheeler, *Shakespeare's Development and the Problem Comedies: Turn and Counter-Turn* (Berkeley and Los Angeles: University of California Press, 1981), 158-59.

12. In *Time and the Artist* Blanpied astutely remarks that Richard "assaults himself by assaulting others" and that the successful mobilization of power against him is evidence of his own power (123).

13. A shorter version of the analysis that follows appeared in my "Psychoanalyzing the Shakespeare Text: The First Three Scenes of the Henriad," in *Shakespeare and the Question of Theory*, ed. Patricia Parker and Geoffrey Hartman (New York: Methuen, 1985), 215.

14. Stephen Booth, "Syntax as Rhetoric in *Richard II*," *Mosaic* 10 (1977): 91. Booth demonstrates what he is describing in this essay with several wittily stuffed sentences, and the fragment crammed into my sentence belongs to one of them.

15. But of course if it were true—or at least if it were common knowledge—that Gaunt was the first holder of the title and duchy, we might suspect another Ricardian irony.

16. Donald Friedman takes this line, arguing that it is "in keeping with Richard's character in the early part of the play that he should mean exactly what he says" ("John of Gaunt and the Rhetoric of Frustration," *English Literary History* 43 [1976]: 298n. 14).

17. Leonard Dean, "*Richard II:* The State and the Image of the Theater," in *Shakespeare: Modern Essays in Criticism*, ed. Dean (orig. pub. 1952; rpt. New York: Oxford University Press, 1961), 162.

18. The previous two sentences and most of the next paragraph are borrowed in slightly altered form from "Psychoanalyzing the Shakespeare Text," 221-22.

19. The words *contrive* and *complot* echo a phrase in Bolingbroke's appeal of Mowbray: the treasons "complotted and contrived in this land" (1.1.95-96). Richard's throwing them back to their first utterer suggests his awareness of the true direction of the appeal.

20. E. M. W. Tillyard, *Shakespeare's History Plays* (London: Chatto and Windus, 1948), 260.

21. Note in *The Second Part of King Henry IV*, ed. A. R. Humphreys, Arden edition (London: Methuen, 1966), 93.

22. Lois Potter, "The Antic Disposition of Richard II," *Shakespeare Survey* 27 (1974): 39, 28. For an example of the view Potter is arguing against see Robert Ornstein, *A Kingdom for a Stage: The Achievement of Shakespeare's History Plays* (Cambridge: Harvard University Press,

1972), 102–24. Ornstein argues that at first Richard is "neither indecisive nor ineffectual" but becomes so because of "his fear and hatred of Bolingbroke" (108). As he falls into helpless incompetence he improves in stature: "calamity makes him wiser and more gracious though less kingly and less capable of rule than before" (118). A similar view is elaborated by Moody E. Prior in *The Drama of Power: Studies in Shakespeare's History Plays* (Evanston, Ill.: Northwestern University Press, 1973), 139–82, especially 168–82.

23. Joseph Porter, *The Drama of Speech Acts: Shakespeare's Lancastrian Tetralogy* (Berkeley and Los Angeles: University of California Press, 1979).

24. Nicholas Brooke, *Shakespeare's Early Tragedies* (orig. pub. 1968; rpt. London: Methuen, 1973), 136, 126.

25. Anne Righter Barton, *Shakespeare and the Idea of the Play* (London: Chatto and Windus, 1962), 124; Ornstein, *A Kingdom for a Stage*, 121; James Calderwood, *Metadrama in Shakespeare's Henriad* (Berkeley and Los Angeles: University of California Press, 1979), 18. Critics who focus selectively on metatheater and metadrama tend to accept Richard's self-representation as his reality rather than as a rhetorical effect, perhaps because it supports their interest in the ontology of role-playing. For another recent example, see Thomas F. Van Laan, *Role-Playing in Shakespeare* (Toronto: University of Toronto Press, 1978), 117–29, especially 124.

26. Stephen Greenblatt, *Renaissance Self-Fashioning: From More to Shakespeare* (Chicago: University of Chicago Press, 1980), 200, 212, 203, 213.

27. For some unsystematic comments on Shakespeare's use of Marlowe, see M. C. Bradbrook, "Shakespeare's Recollections of Marlowe," in *Shakespeare's Styles: Essays in Honor of Kenneth Muir*, ed. Philip Edwards, Inga-Stina Ewbank, and G. K. Hunter (Cambridge: Cambridge University Press, 1980), 183–204, especially 196.

28. For a different reading of the passage, see Murray Schwartz, "Anger, Wounds, and the Forms of Theater in *King Richard II*: Notes for a Psychoanalytic Interpretation," in *Assays: Critical Approaches to Medieval and Renaissance Texts*, vol. 2, ed. Peggy A. Knapp (Pittsburgh: University of Pittsburgh Press, 1983), 115–29. On the narcissistic and self-accusatory aspects of this episode, see Coursen, *Leasing Out of England*, 58. Schwartz ignores the political dimension of the episode and Coursen the demonic seduction of Bolingbroke performed by Richard.

Kantorowicz argues that when "Richard dashes the mirror to the ground, there shatters not only Richard's past and present, but every aspect of a super-world" and "every possibility of a second or super-body" (*The King's Two Bodies*, 40). But what Richard appears to be symbolizing is the brittleness of the glory that must rely on the fragile glassy essence of the human image. The sunny glory of the reflected face is not only "the image of kingship in the early liturgical sense" (39) but also the fiction constructed by Richard's followers. Claudio Guillen mentions "the varying conditions under which King Richard is reduced to acting as a mere *homo exterior* or surrenders to the outer glitter of language, while royalty is no more than an empty role. On those occasions the hero . . . is led . . . to question his face as if it could answer for the disappearing inner being" (*Literature as System: Essays toward the Theory of Literary History* [Princeton: Princeton University Press, 1971], 308). But something like an inner being is never more apparent than at this moment when, like Pilate, he shows "an outward pity" for himself, knowingly misreads the sins inscribed in "the very book" of his kingship, and smashes the mirror he has invested with that misreading. For me, the politics of the play is more intensely centered in the inner being of the body natural than it is for Kantorowicz, and my own reading of the episode owes most to Brooke's sensitive and at times striking analysis of its *ethical* politics, that is, of Richard's campaign to plant the banner of his own guilt and self-despite in Bolingbroke's conscience: see *Shakespeare's Early Tragedies*, 129–34.

29. And also of mockery: "Say that *again?* That's quite complex. Too profound for casual comprehension. Let's slow it down some and look further into it."

30. It might be objected that this sense of *shadow* ("foreshadow") is not found elsewhere in Shakespeare. There is, however, one passage that implies it: the perspective-glass discussion in 2.3. The Queen's response to Bushy's distinction between shadow and substance (14–27) suggests that her present sadness is the shadow of future grief, some "unborn sorrow" that she as yet possesses only "in reversion" (10, 38).

31. The distinction between the two implied morals, public and private—or political and ethicopsychological—was prepared for by the interchange in lines 190–95 of this scene:

> Your cares set up do not pluck my cares down.
> My care is loss of care, by old care done;
> Your care is gain of care, by new care won.
> The cares I give, I have, though given away,
> They 'tend the crown, yet still with me they stay.

Richard will resign his crown and part of his *cares* but will remain king of his *griefs.* Now, in the mirror episode, he generously moves to bequeath or alienate his unseen grief along with his crown and his cares.

CHAPTER FOUR

1. Wolfgang Clemen, *The Development of Shakespeare's Imagery* (Cambridge: Harvard University Press, 1951), p. 55.

2. John Baxter, *Shakespeare's Poetic Styles: Verse into Drama* (London: Routledge and Kegan Paul, 1980), 125–26. Erich Auerbach, *Mimesis: The Representation of Reality in Western Literature,* trans. Willard R. Trask (Princeton: Princeton University Press, 1953), 298. Montaigne's sentence is from 3:13, "Of Experience," in *The Complete Works of Montaigne,* trans. Donald M. Frame (Stanford: Stanford University Press, 1957), 822.

3. Benveniste, *Problems in General Linguistics,* 67.

4. Georges A. Bonnard, "The Actor in Richard II," *Shakespeare-Jahrbuch* 87–88 (1952): 87–101.

5. Sundelson has noted Richard's tendency to regression but ascribes it to Shakespeare's portrait of Richard rather than to Richard's self-representation. Sundelson argues that Richard's play here "is solipsistic—the mother plays with her *own* tears and smiles—and the fantasy is one of fusion rather than attachment. Richard *is* both the mother and the loved, protected child" (*Shakespeare's Restorations,* 39, my italics). The italicized *is* implies commitment to the psychologistic fallacy. Sundelson's readings are often perceptive and sometimes striking, but the general approach his study illustrates is one from which I find it necessary to dissociate my own practice. Sundelson, for example, sees in this passage "a moment of euphoria," a fantasy Richard lives, a "yearning for 'this nurse, this teeming womb'" (38); I see in it a fantasy he plays, or represents, or parodies.

6. For a different reading see Derek Traversi, *Shakespeare: From "Richard II" to "Henry V"* (Stanford: Stanford University Press, 1957), 29–30. My reading of the scene owes much to Traversi's fine-grained and sensitive analysis, but we are ultimately at variance because we situate similar perceptions in different frameworks, which alters their interpretive focus. Thus where Traversi sees "a character too ready to exploit his own emotions" and distracted by an "essentially morbid, febrile imagination" (30), I see a character who *displays* his emotions and who, with wry, bitter amusement, *imposes* his "morbid, febrile" imaginings on his auditors in order to exploit *their* emotions. Traversi's focus is on the *character* performing as an isolate for the benefit of playgoers or readers, rather than on the *speaker* performing for the benefit of onstage interlocutors.

7. See the gloss in *The Life and Death of King Richard the Second,* ed. Matthew W. Black, *A New Variorum Edition of Shakespeare,* vol. 27 (Philadelphia: J. B. Lippincott, 1955), 182.

8. *Macbeth,* 4.3.235.

9. See Verity's reading and the Editor's comment in the Variorum, 182. I partly concur with John Baxter's reading of this phrase: It "introduces a slightly embarrassed and self-conscious apology to the reasonable men whose allegiance he might more profitably have invoked," therefore "'senseless' carries . . . a hint that his conjuration is ultimately

pointless" (*Shakespeare's Poetic Styles*, 123). Baxter's statement, however, that, "despite the apology, he does not really overcome a basic satisfaction with the libertine world of his own conjuring" (123) treats as a moral and psychological failing what I take to be a mocking self-representation offered to his interlocutors.

10. G. R. Hibbard, *The Making of Shakespeare's Dramatic Poetry* (Toronto: University of Toronto Press, 1981), 181. See also the report in the Variorum, 182, that Margaret Webster, directing Maurice Evans's American production, had the interlocutors "whisper and smile among themselves until the king could not help noticing."

In its detail Hibbard's is an extraordinarily fine study from which I continue to learn. My comments here are focused only on the negative effect of his organizing narrative on the clarity of distinctions that have theoretical significance.

11. For Baxter, for example, it is "Shakespeare's golden style" that "absorbs blunt diction, or unpleasant intrusions of reality, into the presiding mood of self-righteous confidence" (129–30). But it makes a difference that the immediate purveyor of this style is Richard, not Shakespeare. Baxter's overall project is a study of Shakespeare's adventures with the plain and golden styles, and the narrative form he gives it is the standard one of development to a "mature style" that reconciles the two (195). This project gets in the way of his ability to read *Richard II* for its own sake, without having to prove that Shakespeare wasn't yet in full control. Consequently he tends to conflate his stylistic critique of Shakespeare with his moral critique of Richard. If "Richard's celebration of Divine Right is little more than a self-protective solipsism elevated to grandiose proportions" (130), it is because Shakespeare self-indulgently ladled out too much golden mead and not enough moral porridge: "Richard's golden style, successful for depicting his own intense feeling, is too free, too private, and too idiosyncratic to enrich his moral understanding" (122).

Baxter's and Hibbard's books were discussed together by George T. Wright in a judicious and genuinely helpful review essay, "Approaches to Shakespeare's Style," *Shakespeare Quarterly* 33 (1982): 111–15.

12. These parallel separations are the subject of many of the studies that connect Richard's theatricality with the loss of a "medieval" ideology in which *res* and *verba* were magically fused. To my knowledge the first attempt to synthesize these themes was made by M. M. Mahood in *Shakespeare's Wordplay* (London: Methuen, 1957), 73–88. Dean's earlier "*Richard II*" focuses more directly on the sociopolitical dimension of the play's theatricality. I find Dean's suggestive if undeveloped comments more helpful than the many subsequent studies that laboriously try to connect Richard's theatricality to the *res/verba* split, as if Shakespeare's language is about Shakespeare's language, or about language as such.

13. Blanpied, *Time and the Artist*. The absence of this linkage mars

Thomas Van Laan's study of *Richard II* in *Role-Playing in Shakespeare,* 117–29. Van Laan astutely catches the accents of histrionic awareness in Richard's apostrophe, noting "the ease and rapidity with which he shifts from one mood to another on cue, as if he were proving his ability to represent in proper rhetorical style each of the various passions." This is an important insight, and I shall return to it later. "There is," he continues, "almost an impression of fakery in Richard's performance, but of course he is not faking. It is simply that his world is so completely a stage that only outward show truly exists for him" (120). Failing to find the textual clues to the particular form of despair and *curiositas* that motivates Richard's performance, Van Laan falls back on the unconditioned—and therefore superficial—metatheatrical explanation: "no longer . . . secure about the role" he played "so flamboyantly" at Coventry, "his discovery that he . . . is merely a player-king . . . is evidently *by itself* sufficient to bring about his deposition" (120–21).

14. "In spite of all" is studiedly unspecific: "God hath power to keep you king (a) 'in spite of all' that happens to you and/or (b) 'in spite of all' you do to undignify and depose yourself."

15. As Traversi puts it, "Richard takes up the assurance whilst neglecting the warning" (*Shakespeare,* 30–31)—not, however, from "an incapacity in the face of practical necessity" (30) but from an interest in staging hyperboles of power that flaunt the incapacity.

16. The first two comments are those of Herford and Coleridge in the Variorum, 184 and 185. The third comment is by James A. S. McPeek, "Richard II and His Shadow World," *American Imago* 15 (1958): 199, and the fourth by S. K. Heninger, Jr., "The Sun-King Analogy in *Richard II*," *Shakespeare Quarterly* 11 (1960): 322.

17. Andrew Gurr, Introduction to his edition of *King Richard II* in *The New Cambridge Shakespeare* (Cambridge: Cambridge University Press, 1984), 27.

18. Discussing the monetary puns, Mahood notes that the "secondary meaning of *worldly*—'mercenary'—provokes a shock of dissent with Richard's trust in his divine right"; might backed by money "is going to make short work of even divine right" (*Shakespeare's Wordplay,* 84), to which I add only that Richard may not be unaware of this dissent, since his language encourages it.

19. Bertrand Evans, *Shakespeare's Tragic Practice* (Oxford: Oxford University Press, 1979), 170.

20. In the chapter on *Richard II* Shakespeare-as-protagonist is brought in only to account for defects in the play. But this motif is central to the book as a whole, and many of Blanpied's critical judgments seem motivated by the need to keep the metatheatrical thesis going.

21. And thus this form of metatheatrical criticism joins hands with the developmental criticism I sampled earlier, and it falls prey to the same structural weaknesses.

22. Blanpied, *Time and the Artist,* 139. See also James L. Calder-

wood, *Shakespearean Metadrama* (Minneapolis: University of Minnesota Press, 1971), 153: "the imagery of the garden scene suggests that both poet-dramatist and poet-king need to discipline their speech to the requirements of stage and state, one of which is incisive action."

23. Blanpied's study is flawed throughout by the unfortunate rhetorical effect of the co-optive "we," embedded in which is the hypothesis of an ideal and unanimous community of readers (and spectators or auditors) created in his image. This plural is unobjectionable when used to distinguish readers or spectators from characters, but not when used to solicit community support for the individual critic's interpretive responses.

24. Bert States, *Great Reckonings in Little Rooms: On the Phenomenology of Theater* (Berkeley and Los Angeles: University of California Press, 1985), 184.

25. This is clearly the case with certain forms of the aside—for example, the comic aside, which, as States observes, "presumes that the audience is in complicity with the setting of traps and deceits" (170)— and with more expansive versions of the "alienation effect" that appear to sacrifice illusion and identification to social critique and irony, distance and control, etc. Metaphysically it makes a difference whether we view this collaborative device as aimed at the actual or the fictional theater audience, though in early modern comedy the practical effect may not be important enough to matter. It does make a practical difference in modernist Brechtian theater, since the positioning of the alienated audience is also a way of representing it (as a synecdoche of the "world" depicted in the onstage fiction), and the appeals to its distance and superiority are ironically juxtaposed to devices that constitute it as no better than the collection of knaves and gulls onstage. In the concluding section of this study, however, I suggest that Shakespearean drama displays proto-Brechtian devices of this sort.

26. My concern in these pages is with Shakespeare's *use* of theater to elucidate or represent aspects of his dramatic fictions. Another kind of metatheatrical criticism explores his *representation* of theater in his dramatic fictions. A superior version of this criticism, shrewd and wide-ranging (if somewhat impressionistic), is to be found in Alvin Kernan's *The Playwright as Magician* and in his "Shakespeare's Stage Audiences."

27. For some interesting comments on the intertextual echoes of soliloquy, see Barton, *Shakespeare's Idea of the Play*, 60–61.

28. Clemen, *Development of Shakespeare's Imagery*, 56; Traversi, *Shakespeare*, 30.

CHAPTER FIVE

1. The comments by Bolingbroke that open 3.3 indicate that the Welsh defectors hadn't yet joined his forces.

2. Variorum, 189.

3. Hardin Craig, cited by Ure in the Arden edition, 98.

4. The Arden edition adopts the "twenty thousand names" of the Quartos, but a survey of the rationalizations offered by commentators in the Variorum (190) yields more than one reason in support of my argument for preferring the Folio's "forty thousand." I am indebted to Beth Pittenger for the idea that generated the following interpretation of the numerical leaps.

5. The comma after "safe" makes the imperative mood more probable but doesn't exclude the indicative sense in which the first clause is bound together as the third-person subject of "fly."

6. This difference may be clearer if expressed by the verbs *to feel* and *to emote;* the latter is more active, more directed, less diffuse.

7. The phrase is Joseph Porter's: *Drama of Speech Acts,* 34.

8. G. L. Kittredge, ed., *The First Part of "King Henry the Fourth"* (Boston: Ginn, 1940), 151.

9. Within the differences between the two Richards there are some odd resemblances. Both display a morbid pleasure in activating what may be called the villain's discourse, whose formula is the inversion of Lear's "I am a man / More sinned against than sinning," i.e., the villain boasts that he is more sinning than sinned against. A. P. Rossiter has remarked of Richard III that he "inhabits a world where everyone deserves everything he can do to them" (*Angels with Horns and Other Shakespeare Lectures,* ed. Graham Story [New York: Longmans, Green, 1961], 16). Richard II is a little more selective in his choice of victims, and what chiefly differentiates him from Richard III is that he acts primarily as if he deserves everything he can do to himself.

10. There is a possible moment of pronominal confusion at "him" which may briefly associate Bolingbroke with God: "If he serve God, we'll serve him as well as God." My friend Paul Whitworth (personal communication) has argued that this is one of several indications that Richard aspires to "clear" himself by purging the crown of both his and Bolingbroke's malfeasance—tossing it, so to speak, beyond both of them.

11. Traversi, *Shakespeare,* 31.

12. Robert Rentoul Reed, Jr., observes that the description suggests "not a disciplined band of warriors but rather a pilgrimage of innocents trudging to the relief of a ravished shrine" (*Crime and God's Judgment in Shakespeare* [Lexington: University of Kentucky Press, 1984], 82–83). In the image "of a mission sanctified by God . . . Shakespeare has provided Bolingbroke's objective with indications of divine approbation," most pointedly signified by the mention of beadsmen. If an aura of this sort surrounds the speech it is important to attribute it to the messenger as well as to Shakespeare. And it makes sense for Scroope to meet Richard's appropriation of religious concepts with a counterthrust

implying that the "favor of Heaven . . . has begun to shift . . . from Richard . . . to Bolingbroke" (83).

13. George Puttenham, *The Arte of English Poesie,* ed. Gladys Doidge Willcock and Alice Walker (orig. pub. 1936; rpt. Cambridge: Cambridge University Press, 1970), 166.

14. Richard could be imagined to respond so quickly as to appear to interrupt Scroope, and the consequence of this surmise is that one supposes Scroope would have continued with his report and therefore is not setting Richard up. The reason I think he *is* represented as setting Richard up is that the addition of the words "with him" to "Peace have they made" is misleading. "Peace have they made indeed, my lord" (but not with him) would more clearly indicate death. Since Scroope is in my view feeding Richard a false clue, I don't think he should appear to be interrupted.

15. The reference to "*spotted* souls" triggers a reminder of Richard's opening apostrophe because it glances not only at the viper but also at the lurking adder and the "heavy-gaited toads" who should have done "annoyance" to the treacherous feet.

16. See Baxter, *Shakespeare's Poetic Styles,* 133–34, for a careful analysis of this modulation.

17. I am grateful to Beth Pittenger for suggesting how the implications of the present perfect in this passage may be associated with Richard's future perfect intentions, which I discuss next.

18. Benveniste, *Problems in General Linguistics,* 210, 212–13. For some pertinent comments on Benveniste's distinctions see Jonathan Culler, *Structuralist Poetics* (Ithaca: Cornell University Press, 1975), 197–200.

19. The reference to Senecan "ghosts" directs the allusion to Shakespeare's play, since in Holinshed the ghosts are devils Richard only dreams about.

20. See J. LaPlanche and J.-B. Pontalis, *The Language of Psycho-Analysis,* trans. Donald Nicholson-Smith (New York: Norton, 1973), 477–78.

21. See Catherine Clément's interesting observations on the use of the future perfect—or future anterior—in Freudian and Lacanian psychoanalysis: *The Lives and Legends of Jacques Lacan,* trans. Arthur Goldhammer (New York: Columbia University Press, 1983), 122–23. That the future perfect operates there between the past and the present, while it operates between present and future in the passage I am dealing with, bears out Benveniste's argument about its chronological openness.

22. Baxter, *Shakespeare's Poetic Styles,* 136.

23. "A king"—any particular king—rather than "*the* king" (or "this king") maintains Richard's distance and detachment from the emblem.

24. Barton, *Shakespeare and the Idea of the Play,* 116.

25. Potter, "Antic Disposition," 40.

26. Mahood, *Shakespeare's Wordplay*, 85.

27. Coursen, *Leasing Out of England*, 51; Baxter, *Shakespeare's Poetic Styles*, 134–35; Traversi, *Shakespeare*, 32.

28. Baxter, *Shakespeare's Poetic Styles*, 136. See also his rebuke to Richard on 90.

29. Jean-Paul Sartre, *The Emotions: Outline of a Theory*, trans. Bernard Frechtman (New York: Philosophical Library, 1948), 90.

30. At least one often-noted problem caused by the concept, its essentialism, could be avoided by replacing the notion of "consciousness" with the more recent French notion of "the subject" constructed and situated in specific ideological or discursive formations.

31. Berthold Brecht, "Alienation Effects in Chinese Acting," in *Brecht on Theatre*, trans. John Willett (New York: Hill and Wang, 1964), 94–95.

32. Porter, *Drama of Speech Acts*, 33.

Epilogue

1. Stanley Fish, *Is There a Text in This Class? The Authority of Interpretive Communities* (Cambridge: Harvard University Press, 1980), 200.

2. John Langshaw Austin, *How to Do Things with Words*, ed. J. O. Urmson and Maria Sbisa, 2d ed. (Cambridge: Harvard University Press, 1975), 155–57.

3. See Fish, *Is There a Text in This Class?*, 231, and "With the Compliments of the Author," 712–21.

4. *2 Henry IV*, 3.1.31. This is Henry's first appearance and speech in the play. It had been preceded by several references to his illness, including Falstaff's knowing diagnosis: "It hath it original from much grief, from study, and perturbation of the brain; . . . it is a kind of deafness" (1.2.114–16). In Henry's next long speech, with its acknowledgment of the truth of Richard's prophecy (3.1.45–79), the anxiety displaced from the surface of the insomnia soliloquy breaks through.

5. Terence Hawkes, "Postscript: Theater against Shakespeare," in *The Elizabethan Theater: Papers Given at the International Conference on Elizabethan Theater Held at the University of Waterloo, Ontario in July 1968*, ed. David Galloway (London: Macmillan, 1969), 125. Hawkes's essay was the closing commentary. See his *Shakespeare's Talking Animals* (London: Edward Arnold, 1973) for an expanded treatment of the ideas discussed in this brief occasional essay.

6. Michael Bristol, "Carnival and the Institutions of Theater in Elizabethan England," *English Literary History* 50 (1983): 646. See also Bristol's expansion of the thesis of this essay in his equally stimulat-

ing *Carnival and Theater: Plebeian Culture and the Structure of Authority in Renaissance England* (New York: Methuen, 1985).

7. M. C. Bradbrook, *The Rise of the Common Player: A Study of Actor and Society in Shakespeare's England* (Cambridge: Harvard University Press, 1962), 40, 42, 100.

8. Ann Jennalie Cook, *The Privileged Playgoers of Shakespeare's London, 1576–1642* (Princeton: Princeton University Press, 1981). See the criticism of Cook by Martin Butler in *Theatre and Crisis 1632–1642* (Cambridge: Cambridge University Press, 1984). Butler argues that the number of unprivileged London playgoers was much more significant than Cook allows.

9. Richard Levin, "'Shakespeare's Second Globe,'" *Times Literary Supplement*, 25 January 1974, 81.

10. Stephen Orgel, *The Illusion of Power: Political Theater in the English Renaissance* (Berkeley and Los Angeles: University of California Press, 1975), 8–9.

11. Barry Weller, "Identity and Representation in Shakespeare," *English Literary History* 49 (1982): 342.

12. Greenblatt, "Invisible Bullets," 42–44.

Index

Compositor: G & S Typesetters, Inc.
Text: 10/12 Sabon
Display: Sabon
Printer: Braun-Brumfield, Inc.
Binder: Braun-Brumfield, Inc.